M000281963

"When I read this b
Annette wrote this, s. ~~~ ~~~ ~~~ if you pick at your skin and it causes you distress, I highly recommend that you read this personable - and highly practical - book about living with, and healing from Skin Picking Disorder *(Excoriation Disorder)*. In sharing her own pathway to freedom, Annette has outlined a tremendously useful approach that can be implemented and/or adapted by anyone motivated enough to do the footwork."

> \- **Christina Pearson**, President, Heart and Soul Academy, Inc.
> Founder, Trichotillomania Learning Center *(1990 - 2013)*

"Annette Pasternak's book, *Skin Picking: the Freedom to Finally Stop*, is a comprehensive, holistic guide for changing pathological skin picking behavior. Dr. Pasternak eloquently combines her personal experience with behavioral solutions, cognitive interventions, and biological alternatives (diet, exercise, meditation, self-care) to help readers heal from this difficult condition. I will enthusiastically recommend this book to my clients who suffer with both skin picking and other body-focused repetitive behaviors."

> \- **Suzanne Mouton-Odum, Ph.D.**, co-author of
> *A Parent Guide to Hair Pulling Disorder*

"Filled with wisdom and experience, *Skin Picking* is a gift to those who suffer from skin picking disorder. Readers will not only feel less alone but genuinely hopeful as Pasternak lays out a realistic plan for recovery from this devastating disorder."

> \- **Claudia Miles, M.A., LMFT**

"There are tragically few books for skin pickers. I celebrate the appearance of this honest and clear account of the approaches that have helped Annette recover from skin picking, and which she now uses in her own work with coaching clients. Annette rightfully makes clear that recovery requires long term, hard work - and there is no single answer for all of us. But she supports the reader with encouragement and concrete tools to make the process less daunting. Most important of all is the key message of the book - hope."

> \- **Jennifer Raikes**, Executive Director,
> Trichotillomania Learning Center, Inc.

Skin Picking

The Freedom to Finally Stop

Annette Pasternak, Ph.D.
with Tammy Fletcher, M.A., L.M.F.T

Copyright © 2014 Annette Pasternak

Contents

Author's Note

The self-help advice in this book is meant to be educational and is not intended as a substitute for psychotherapy, nutritional counseling, medical care or spiritual guidance. Please seek the appropriate professionals when needed.

We are all individuals with different circumstances, health concerns and sensitivities to food and supplements. I advise you to consult a health professional before taking supplements or implementing any of the other information in this book. I do not promise results and I accept no liability.

Section 1 - Introductory Material

Welcome

Congratulations! Please give yourself an appreciative pat on the back. Beginning to read this book is an important first step toward freedom from chronic, ongoing and destructive skin picking. Chances are you have had a skin picking problem for a very long time and have tried very very hard to get yourself to **not** do the behavior, to no avail. Any amount of effort you have tried and perhaps succeeded at, temporarily, you have ultimately gone back to picking with a sense of hopelessness that you will ever be free of this compulsion.

Having been there myself, I completely understand. But from now on, I want you to think, "No more hopelessness." Simply trust that it can be done, and from now on, focus on learning how and taking positive steps. When you focus on hopelessness and doubt, that only causes the hopelessness to grow. You've already done that enough, haven't you? Did you know that if you look at a wall by the side of the freeway instead of the lane you are in, you will likely drive into that wall? (Don't test it!) I know where you want to be – you want to have perfect skin and feel great and be 100% skin picking-free. But if you look at that as the only acceptable place to be, and you see how far you are from that reality, you're not going to be able to do it. Yet I know you *are* capable of taking small positive steps and being okay with gradual progress, and with where you are at each moment along the way. Starting now, see if you can open yourself up to being okay with how you are right now. Because only when we are focused on *now* do we have the power to choose, and each choice we make *now* determines our future. When you make peace with now, you will get a future that is bright with all the possibilities you deserve.

Chances are, if you are a skin picker, you are also a perfectionist. Know that perfectionism is your enemy, more than the skin picking is. You can even look at the picking as a symptom of the perfectionism. Nobody is perfect, and if you continually strive for perfection, you will never measure up, and the thought of being "less than" will make you miserable.

When I was 28 years old, my friends and I went hiking in the Grand Canyon, and stayed overnight at the bottom of the canyon at Phantom Ranch. One of the rangers, in her talk that night, told us that the next day when we hike out of the canyon, the rim of the canyon would always look so far away. For nearly the entire day, it would never appear any closer, and with our tired legs, we might feel discouraged. But then she told us the secret to staying motivated. "When you get tired," she said, "turn around and look behind you, and you will see all the trail behind you, winding back and forth, this way and that. You'll see you *have* actually made some progress towards the top. You *are* actually getting somewhere, step by step." She was right. The whole hike out of the canyon the next day, the canyon rim looked so far away, so high up, like it wasn't ever getting closer. But we saw a lot of progress looking back, progress we couldn't see in the process of slowly trudging forward on our increasingly tired legs.

Looking constantly at the "canyon rim" when we have a long way to go is not fruitful. It is better to get satisfaction from merely putting one foot in front of the other, even at those times when we are tired of the whole journey. We need to take satisfaction in knowing that all we need to take care of right now is simply walking uphill, rather than down. We need to trust that walking continually uphill inevitably gets us to where we want to go.

So, as you do the work in this book, see if you can take satisfaction in the fact that you *are* taking positive steps. And focus on that, rather than feeling you don't measure up, or how much further you have to go to stop your skin picking, or to heal your scars. Trust that it can be done, make up your mind that you will do it, and then bit by bit, go boldly forward on the path ahead.

Who am I? How do I help skin pickers and why have I written this book?

I am a holistic health coach, and since that is a relatively new profession, I will explain a little more about it, and in what ways I am qualified and what ways I am less qualified than others who help people like you who pick their skin.

Health coaching is a relatively new and rapidly growing profession. It is filling a great need for helping patients implement healing diet and lifestyle changes, subjects in which medical doctors both receive little training in, and have little time for.

Medical doctors have a lot on their plate. Due to the structuring of insurance, they often have only a few minutes to spend with each patient. In such a small window of time, they cannot possibly provide all the support a person facing an illness, disease or disorder needs. Frequently, illnesses and conditions respond remarkably well (often better than drugs) to natural interventions like changing the persons diet, and it takes a lot longer to help a person learn to change their eating habits than a doctor has in those few minutes. Most doctors don't know the diet and lifestyle changes that are appropriate for every disease and disorder they treat.

This is where health coaches come in. There are holistic health coaches specializing in probably every health problem that exists, from diabetes, cancer and heart disease, to thyroid conditions, autoimmune diseases and eating disorders.

Holistic health coaches are trained in counseling and often work with populations and health problems similar to the ones they've suffered from, so they may have a natural connection to their clients that the doctor would not. They also know that, in addition to the food we eat, relationships, spirituality and the work we do also can have profound effects on our health. These areas often affect our health more than what we eat.

If you have any doubt about the truth of that statement, I refer you to the research summarized in the recent book "Mind over Medicine" by Lissa Rankin, M.D.[1] which clearly shows the primary importance of factors usually considered secondary to our health (or not even considered), such as our relationships and spiritual life. Also in the book, Dr. Rankin makes the case for the importance of the health care provider's time spent caring for the patient's health, and the caring manner in which the doctor treats the patient. She points out that the placebo effect in clinical trials (where a certain number of people are not getting the tested drug treatment, and nobody knows whether they are getting it or not) is due to the healing effects of the caring attitude and time spent with the patients on the project. The patient feels relaxed and reassured instead of stressed and upset, which provides a state enabling healing.

By extending this concept, merely talking to and being in the presence of a therapist or coach is healing. Having someone pay attention to you and your problems in a caring way is already starting the healing process.

Currently, health coaches are not licensed professionals. We do not have the requirement of hours of supervision by experienced coaches that licensed therapists and counselors have. We receive one year of training and are on our own, so it is very much up to the individual to consider whether the coach is trustworthy as far as providing quality service. We are not the ones to see if you have serious psychological problems - those issues that go beyond skin picking and non-debilitating amounts of depression and anxiety. Or at least not the ones to see as your sole source of help. We can be part of your healing team. For example, I have clients who go to mental health professionals concurrently with seeing me. Sometimes those professionals have referred their patients to me for the more specific help that I can offer.

At the time of writing this book, I have seen twenty individual clients for skin picking (some of these I am still seeing). Nearly all have been thrilled with the results they've achieved with the assistance of my coaching. I fully acknowledge that this is a small number for someone who has the audacity to write a book on the subject. There are at least a few psychologists around who have seen perhaps hundreds of clients for skin picking, and no doubt they would write a different book than me, if they decided to write a book on this topic.

Yet there is a great need for this book. This is a niche that has not been filled. At the time of this writing, there is no other self-help book solely dedicated to the skin picking problem.

There are a few self-help type books on the topic of hair pulling that would be helpful to someone with a skin picking disorder, assuming the person would know to look there. Much of the material in Section 2 of this book is derived from "The Hair-Pulling Problem" by Fred Penzel, Ph.D. Another good book for self-help is "Help for Hair Pullers" by Nancy J. Keuthen, Ph.D., Dan J. Stein, MD and Gary A. Christenson, M.D. Other books with information for skin pickers specifically can be counted on one hand. The only ones of which I'm aware are "Pearls: Meditations on Recovery from Hair Pulling and Skin Picking" by Christina Sophia Pearson, "The Habit Change Workbook" by James Claiborn, Ph.D. ABPP and Cherry Pedrick, R.N., and "Skin Deep" by Ted A. Grossbart, Ph.D. and Carl Sherman, Ph.D.

This is very much the book I wanted to write. I know for many of you, it will be exactly the book you long to read. For others of you, particularly if you are not open to "alternative" approaches to health, or if you have more faith in the scientific process and western medicine than you have in a higher power, parts of it may not be your cup of tea. I hope you will find it helpful anyway.

Here are the major influences to my approach: I draw on the cognitive behavioral therapy (CBT) techniques used in the hair pulling books mentioned above, as well as by what I learned in the skin picking and hair pulling therapy group at the OCD Center of Los Angeles. I am influenced by the varied approaches to wellness I learned during my health coach training at the Institute for Integrative Nutrition (IIN).

I also read widely on topics of self-help, the brain-body connection, spirituality, diet and holistic health, especially Eastern systems, mainly Traditional Chinese Medicine (TCM) and Ayurveda. I am also influenced by my work as a Brain Gym* Instructor/Consultant*.

I have benefited from these systems in my own health, and I have seen TCM at work through Brain Gym, Touch for Health and Emotional Freedom Technique, all of which are based (at least in part) upon TCM concepts of meridians and acupressure points.

I am also influenced by my work coaching individuals who pick their skin and learning from their experiences with these tools.

Probably the biggest influence, a true lifesaver as far as stabilizing my mind and creating a large degree of peace and contentment and the life I have today, has been Yoga - not only the postures, but the breathing techniques, meditation, philosophy and devotional practices.

---

* Brain Gym® is a registered trademark of Brain Gym® International

So this is a different book than others would write. However, I think those differences are its strengths, not only the holistic viewpoint but also the friendly, reassuring tone that comes from having walked this path myself. Now, if you are ready, follow me.

More about a holistic approach to stopping picking

A holistic view considers skin picking to be a symptom of a whole system that is out of balance. Chances are you have other health conditions, whether they are mental or physical, such as depression, anxiety, autoimmune disorders, allergies, headaches, sleeping problems, overweight, disordered eating, problems associated with your menstrual cycle or with menopause. Even if the skin picking is the thing that bothers you the most right now, these are all symptoms of a body out of balance.

Treatment in a holistic way considers the whole person, including the physical, mental/emotional and spiritual aspects of his or her life. The mind has a powerful effect on the body, and the body likewise has a tremendous effect on the mind. A holistic approach honors that, and recognizes that working from all aspects of the problem has a synergistic effect, resulting in quicker and more complete stopping of your skin picking, as well as feeling better overall. Holistic includes your environment, your relationships with your family, friends and significant others, the work you do or your schooling, plus what you eat, how you think, and other aspects of

12

your lifestyle, such as the quality and quantity of exercise and sleep you get.

In my holistic health coaching practice, holistic also means that I use and recommend whatever *works*. It took me a lot of approaches and time to reverse *my* skin picking. It is a persistent problem and reducing picking is a gradual process that takes persistence. It is true that if I knew then what I know now, it would have taken me *less* time. Lucky for you, by reading this book and diligently doing the work required, you can benefit from all that I know now. I'm not going to say it is easy, and I won't promise that you will be able to do it all on your own. There is tremendous value in working with someone who can offer you support, motivation, a tailored approach as well as troubleshooting and seeing your "blind spots." That said, I am astonished that "Skin Picking: The Freedom to Finally Stop" is the first real self-help book published on this topic. Because there is a tremendous amount of self-help work you can do, and it is possible that you *will* be able to do it on your own. What I can promise you is that, if you diligently apply the techniques I am teaching you here, you *will* make progress. Quite possibly you will progress to the point where you feel satisfied and, like me, any minor amount of picking you do will be such a small part of your life that it won't even trouble you anymore. The work I suggest in this book is doable and worthwhile, and in doing it, you will experience benefits far exceeding just stopping your skin picking, including greater health, happiness, internal power and peace.

If you don't do anything about your skin picking, chances are it will get worse. It is like a groove in your mind. The deeper and wider the groove gets, the more your actions will continue to fall into the same behavioral groove. Like a hiking path, the more it is traveled the more established it gets and the more unlikely that anybody but the most daring individuals will venture off the beaten path. When you are in the process of stopping skin picking, you will have to learn to be that adventurer, not once but all the time, because the path will be not just a path, but like a riverbed in the bottom of a canyon. You have to climb your way out of the steep canyon. Right now I assume you have no idea how. Someone has to teach you how to rock climb. It will be treacherous, so at first you may not feel like you are making any progress. You may feel like you are still at the bottom of the riverbed. But if you practice hard enough, you will learn how to get out. It will be hard work, but you will make progress if you are motivated. Make up your mind that you will stop skin picking, and you will. But it will take time. You are learning a challenging skill, like rock-climbing, and you will, at times, fall. When you are not vigilant and neglect to use the tools that I teach you, you will fall. Even at first when you ARE using the tools, you will fall. Rock-climbing is hard. Stopping skin picking is hard. Is that any reason to feel badly about yourself? NO.

There may be a part of you, of which you are not conscious, that may hinder your progress simply because the thought of stopping skin picking is too threatening. That part of you enjoys picking and does not want you to stop. So, for now, let's aim at reducing your skin picking rather than stopping it. Eventually perhaps you'll stop, but for now it will be helpful to learn to be happy with making progress and steadily reducing the picking.

How much time will it take me to stop picking?

Like I said, it does take time. How much time will be related to how motivated you are to stop, how much effort you put into stopping, how entrenched your picking is in the first place, how persistent you are in using the techniques that will help you stop, and how gentle yet firm you are with yourself. There may even be physiologically distinct kinds of skin picking that take different lengths of time and they may respond to different treatment approaches. For example, in my experience most skin pickers do the behavior daily, sometimes only to a moderate extent. But there are people who go for days or weeks without doing it, and then all of a sudden have an extremely damaging episode.

Christina Pearson, the founder of the Trichotillomania Learning Center who, many years ago, struggled with both hair pulling and skin picking and completely recovered from both, says that for a long-term skin picker, it takes a couple of years or more.[2] If picking is a more recent occurrence for you, you may be luckier. One of my clients who had only begun picking in her thirties, and picked for only two years, completely stopped in a matter of months, even though she was picking for hours a day at the start of her coaching program.

The ultimate answer to this question is: I can't really tell you how long it will take you to stop picking or reduce it to the point where it is no longer a problem. In all likelihood you are embarking on a long journey. But once you begin to see progress, chances are good that you'll start to enjoy the process of continually improving as a result of your own efforts.

Do you need therapy for this, and if so, what you can expect?

What is right for you: therapy or self-help? If we are talking either/or, ideally therapy is better. You get personalized help and ongoing support. But you may have reasons for reading this book with the hope that you will be able to overcome your skin picking problem on your own. You may have limited financial resources, for example, or no access to qualified therapists in your area who know how to treat skin picking. You may feel too ashamed or uncomfortable to talk to anyone about your behavior. Or perhaps you are lucky enough to have a milder skin picking condition, one that bothers you enough to want to apply simple self-help efforts, but that is not a big enough issue for you to want to undertake therapy.

If you are in therapy and find that your therapist is helpful, but not with your skin picking, it may help to share this book with them. Perhaps they can be a support for you as you work through it.

Therapy and Skin Picking
By Tammy Fletcher, M.A., Licensed Marriage and Family Therapist

One of the most vital questions to ask any new psychotherapy patient is "Why did you choose to seek support through therapy?" and also, "Why now?" In my work over the last eight years with patients who want to reduce or eliminate skin picking behaviors, these questions let me know many things about the person. Are they motivated to stop? Did someone convince them to give therapy a try? Have they been in therapy before?

All of the above information helps me begin to understand my new patient's reasons for being there with me. Skin picking is a complex issue, and while some of the behaviors may be the same, no two clients are alike. Some commonalities I notice: patients have been in therapy before, and it has not been as helpful as it could be. It can be hard to find a therapist who specializes in Body-Focused Repetitive Behaviors (BFRBs), who will take the time to uncover all the factors which have led to, and now perpetuate, the behavior. Unfortunately, there still remains some confusion in our field as to how to get away from jumping to diagnostic conclusions based on what we have been trained to look for. Obsessive Compulsive Disorder, Attention Deficit and Hyperactivity Disorder, and anxiety are some of the diagnoses most commonly linked with dermatillomania (another name for skin picking disorder). However, it is imperative to go beyond these labels and reveal how chronic skin picking plays a part in each individual's life. Once we do this – and it can take some time working together to identify factors such as negative thought patterns, for example – we can create a treatment plan as unique as the patients themselves.

Oftentimes, dermatillomania affects the entire family. When a loved one struggles with chronic skin picking, it can be problematic for parents, siblings, and significant others. In these cases, seeing a psychotherapist for family therapy can be helpful in a number of ways. If a son or daughter picks, for example, parents can learn how to be supportive without adding to their child's anxiety or shame. In family therapy sessions, we talk candidly about what the person with dermatillomania needs for support. Generally, they respond best to love and acceptance, rather than being singled out as "the family member with the problem." Family therapy allows everyone to express their needs in a safe, contained environment. As parents, we naturally want to intervene to help our children – even as adults – manage their problems. In most cases, just expressing support and faith in the child's ability to eliminate the habit of skin picking is far more beneficial than constant reminding, nagging, or monitoring the behavior. A professional therapist can help get the family back on track, which increases the likelihood of success.

Successful therapy requires more than creativity and openness on the part of the clinician. In my experience, the client's readiness for change is a key factor in determining success in reducing or eliminating skin picking. It can be frightening to give up a habit which has, at some point, possibly provided a distraction or sense of calm. Patients who report picking at the end of a long work day, or after an argument with a spouse, can attest to the relief of "zoning out." When they come to therapy, chances are clients have decided that enough is enough. They want a life free of picking, and they may have tried many times to stop on their own. Part of my job is to support each client in identifying more preferred behaviors and activities which can provide that same sense of calm, distraction, and relief from stress.

Most of my BFRB patients are more interested in focusing on solutions for their present concerns than digging deep into childhood issues and traumas. That said, those old issues may rise to the surface as we work together, and we face them together as they do. A positive outcome in therapy, for any issue, requires a collaborative approach. This is the client's path. I am honored to walk it with them, and to point out pitfalls and tools for change along the way. But ultimately, it is their journey.

I would be remiss if I didn't mention factors that can impede progress in recovery from chronic skin picking. When a client tells me, "I don't want to track my picking, or note my thoughts. Just make it stop," I know they may not be ready. I believe therapy is an active process, requiring participation and commitment from everyone involved. I provide an abundance of resources, activities, and homework to keep the focus on a healthier, pick-free week. In session, we use traditional talk therapy, Cognitive Behavioral and Narrative Therapy, meridian tapping, and hypnotherapy. Successful outcomes are more likely when the client embraces the challenge and trusts the process. Believe me, this is not easy. Ending the habit of compulsive skin picking can be difficult, especially in the beginning. But it can be done!

How to use this book

We are all individuals, with differences, and so each of you may choose to use this book differently. When I coach individuals to stop picking, at the outset I usually follow a certain order of what we do together and what I ask them to do for "homework." However, sometimes I do vary the order of techniques when I feel there is a greater need to address certain aspects of the person's skin picking problem sooner rather than later. Although some of you may be in therapy for your picking, in presenting the topics of this book, I am going with the assumption that you will be working on your own to stop picking, using this book as your guide. You could read and use this book sequentially in the order it is presented, but please know that you can do the work in these chapters concurrently, or even out of order if you feel that may be best for you. You may immediately jump in and do the work involved, or you may prefer to read through the whole book first, and apply what you learned as you see fit. The sections will be synergistic, each containing keys to further unlock the doors standing in the way of stopping picking. Using one may make it easier to employ some of the others.

You may not need to use every one of these techniques and tips to stop picking, or you may need more than a self-help book in order to stop picking. However, you won't know which techniques help you until you try them. And you certainly will not make much progress if you only read the book without doing any of the work.

You are currently reading the introductory section of the book, which will explain all about what skin picking is and why we do it, ways in which it is treated clinically and also the holistic self-help approach we will take here. You have already read a bit about my approach in general as a holistic health coach, as well as some words on how to differentiate whether you may need medical or psychological treatment, as opposed to a coach or a support group. This section also includes my story - my history with skin picking, how it developed and how I began to heal and get it under control.

Following the intro section, Section 2, "Breaking the Habit," is next because it is the basis of what you will be doing when you are ready to stop picking in an active way, and you can start this work right away if you like. The chapters in Section 2 will help you get clear on the effects of your skin picking and your motivations to stop, and they will teach you how to increase your awareness of your skin picking in all its details. Section 2 will also teach you targeted strategies and explain how to use them to help you gain control of your picking and to "loosen" the habit of your behavior. Using the log and the other strategies in this section of the book will most likely give you confidence and hope, as you should see an immediate decrease in the amount you are picking. These strategies may not be enough, long term, because they do not address imbalance in the body and the mind, so you will still feel a need to pick and/or do other unhealthy behaviors.

Section 3 is about changing the way you think and feel about yourself and your picking. This section is very powerful. If you are in total despair, you may want to read and work on Section 3 first. It will give you the positive energy and momentum that will then enable you to tackle Section 2 with more success.

Section 4 is about calming, focusing and grounding techniques. These are the techniques that will give you long-term success by reducing your need to do the skin picking behavior in the first place. They are powerful natural anti-anxiety methods. They also work by further increasing your awareness and ability to be in the present moment, so you can accept whatever discomfort you may feel, emotionally or physically, without resorting to your primary comfort behavior, the picking.

In Section 5, you will find more keys to reducing your skin picking urges by making sure your physiology is in balance. Section 5 is about making changes in your diet and adding helpful supplements. When I coach, I often don't start clients off on diet changes and supplements right away, because I think it's valuable for them to see the results they can get through their own efforts with the techniques introduced earlier in the book, despite the urges they have. However, if you are desperate to reduce your picking as soon as possible, you may want to take a quick look at the beginning of the diet section, the part that talks about sugar, and at the supplements section. Perhaps you will decide to cut down your sugar intake or choose to try a supplement like NAC or 5-HTP right away. These are quick fixes which can make a big difference in your skin picking. Or in the case of NAC, something that may work over time for you as you start on the suggestions in the rest of the book.

Section 6 gathers two more chapters on topics which affect some skin pickers (acne and hormones) and one last chapter on motivation, which applies to everyone.

A note to parents and significant others

Perhaps you do not have a skin picking problem yourself, but have bought this book in order to help a loved one, perhaps one of your children or a partner. You want to help them. Of course you do. However, they are surely sensitive about their skin picking, and any comments you make, they may interpret as criticism and disapproval of who they are, and of the work they may *or may not* be doing in their efforts to stop picking. It is quite possible they may not be ready to stop yet, and if they are not motivated from within themselves, no amount or kind of external motivation from you is going to work. And it may even do damage, certainly to your relationship with them.

I know it hurts to see someone you love suffer. And I know how badly you want to make it all better and do whatever you can to help them stop the damage they are doing to themselves. But the truth remains that you cannot do the work for them, and you cannot get *them* to do the work before they are ready to. I know this truth can be difficult to accept, but accepting this is essential to your peace of mind. And when you do not accept it, chances are that you are putting undue and unhelpful pressure on your loved one.

Be mindful of how you introduce a loved one to this book. Asking them if they would be interested in reading a book on this topic is more respectful than telling them you think they should read it, or just giving it to them. Also, it may be best to resist the temptation to ask questions about it later, such as whether they're reading it, doing the exercises, etc. If they want to do it, they will, when they are ready. And if they want to tell you about it, they probably will. But if you bring it up, they are likely to feel pressured and resist. Especially (but not exclusively) with teenagers, the more obviously important to you it appears that they read the book or stop picking, the *less* likely it will be to happen. If they feel as if they would be stopping picking of their own volition, rather than for you, they will read the book, benefit from it, and be happy that you found it for them.

Why do we pick and how do we stop?

Some skin picking is normal and to some extent almost universal. Nearly everyone will pop an odd pimple, flake off a bit of dry skin, peel the remnants of a sunburn, or trim a hangnail. Animals tend to do it too – they bite at their skin or fur when it is irritated. We like to "fix" things, smooth them out, remove what doesn't seem to belong. To the normal extent that we do these behaviors, they serve a grooming purpose, and have persisted because they have some evolutionary benefit, probably either making us more attractive to the opposite sex or protecting us from infection.

Why did such a normal behavior get out of hand and become a problem for some of us? There are different explanations for why, none of which have been validated scientifically, so we can only guess.

Is it genetic? A study of twins shows that there is a sizable genetic component to skin picking disorder, but there is also a big environmental component.[3] So, it is genetic, yet genetic is hardly ever the hard and fast, set-in-stone cause of things that we would like to believe it is. It is the sole cause of only a very few conditions in the absence of environmental factors. You may be genetically predisposed to a condition but that does not mean you are powerless over it. It does not necessarily mean that you will develop it unless conditions are ripe, and it does not mean that you can't change your conditions to get rid of it. With skin picking, even when you get your system in balance and learn healthy ways to reduce stress and deal with emotions, you still will have a strong habit to break, because you have been doing it for so long.

What is probably the simplest and most accurate explanation is that it is a way of self-soothing, a way to deal with stress and anxiety. While we do it, it temporarily reduces discomfort. But what is causing the anxiety? Is it the external conditions of your life? Or the way your mind responds?

Most people do not know that the food we eat can significantly contribute to anxiety and depression. Food is the grossest influencer of both our physical and mental state. I cannot overstate how important it is that you eat appropriately. Even if you think you are eating healthily, you may not be eating appropriately for your body at this point in time. Your body may have been out of balance for years, but you can get it back in balance, in part by feeding it well, and reduce your body's need to pick in order to regulate itself.

Anxiety is also caused by the more subtle aspects of life than food, such as the way we habitually breathe and the way we habitually think. As young children we learn from our parents unconsciously, without question, almost by osmosis. Anxiety can be passed down from them. We learn to think the way they think about life, and absorb how fearful, worried, nervous or depressed they are. Perhaps you were even abused, neglected or simply not soothed and comforted enough as a child, and as a result, your brain developed in such a way that it did not develop pathways to allow you to soothe and comfort yourself. Instead it developed in such a way that you automatically perceive things fearfully. You will learn techniques in this book to calm yourself naturally, reducing anxiety and re-training your brain to respond to life in a calmer, less threatened, manner. You will also learn how to change your thinking, as you likely have thought habits that contribute to your picking.

Philosophically, the most basic and understandable explanation for skin picking, as well as other body-focused repetitive behaviors (BFRBs) like hair pulling, nail biting or lip chewing, as well as other bad habits and addictions, is that they are ultimately caused by the natural, universal human tendency to avoid pain and discomfort on the one hand, and to seek and gravitate toward pleasure on the other.

This is our human nature, and it is also deep-seated animal behavior. Even the simplest one-celled organisms move away from chemical irritants and toward tasty nutrients.

pain → → pleasure

The problem is, we are so smart that we learn quickly. For example, at one point we learned that picking our skin felt good, or eased a bad feeling we had, even one as mild as slight anxiety. So we did it again. And again... Most likely we did it hundreds or thousands of times before we realized it was a problem for us. By the time we did realize it, it was a habitual behavior that had put down deep roots and had thus become very difficult to break. We tried and tried on our own to stop picking, and failed and failed again. Then, we most likely began to feel badly about ourselves, both because we made our skin look bad and because we felt we should be able to stop, yet were not able to. Soon our negative thoughts about ourselves became another bad habit.

Remember: You are not your skin picking.

You are not any habit or disorder or addiction that you may have. There is nothing wrong with *you*. You simply have a challenging habit to break. This habit is merely your way of expressing the very human tendency of going toward pleasure and avoiding pain. Perhaps you wish you had somebody else's way, but probably if you thought about it you wouldn't. Most of us have one or more ways of falling into the "avoid pain, pursue pleasure" trap that is a natural human tendency.

We human beings are complicated. Our systems function in a very delicate balance. We are thrown out of balance by many things – we may be off kilter physically, by our diet, for example. Or medicines. Certain stimulant medications for ADD have been known to cause skin picking in some individuals. Strong persistent emotions affect us, as does avoiding feeling emotions. In fact, it is possible the picking began in the first place in order to avoid facing an unpleasant emotional truth. Were we loved well enough as children? Were we picked on at home or at school? We may have begun picking in order to avoid the pain of fully feeling an emotional response. Perhaps it was not safe for us to express particular emotions. Maybe we were angry at someone close to us, but were taught we "shouldn't" be angry or express anger. Emotions not fully felt have a strong effect on the body, and picking could start as emotion turned inward.

Or maybe it had nothing to do with avoiding negative emotions or sensations; it was just something fun and exciting that we got hooked on. Perhaps whatever we were sensing with any of our five senses was gratifying. Our brains released pleasure chemicals, including dopamine, which caused us to seek out the biochemical high and reinforce learning of the behavior.

Whatever the cause, it was learned and learned very well. Whether we saw a parent do it or discovered it on our own, we did it enough times that our system learned that this was the way to make ourselves feel better. A learned behavior, like walking, becomes unconscious - we don't need to think about it anymore to do it. It didn't change things that picking eventually made us feel worse, because when it did, we knew unconsciously we could always use it to feel better again. The skin picking has become so automatic for us that the opposite, breaking the habit, will require much energy and effort. In fact, we could say it is not even possible to "break" a habit at all. It's hard or maybe impossible to unlearn something like that, in the same way that it may not be possible to unlearn riding a bicycle! Instead we need to make *new* habits to gradually replace the skin picking.

What is known scientifically?

Not a lot. Even though it affects many individuals, some in a devastating way. Sufferers have been generally ashamed and secretive about it, and the large majority of dermatologists and mental health professionals have been at a loss knowing how to treat it. As a result, it has been somewhat of a hidden subject and consequently has not yet been well-studied scientifically. In fact, it has only been officially recognized by the field of psychiatry in America in the Diagnostic and Statistical Manual of Mental Disorders (DSM) in the year 2013.

In the current version, DSM-5, which debuted in 2013, problematic skin picking is named "excoriation (skin picking) disorder," a relatively innocuous term compared to the other names that have been used in the scientific literature, such as neurotic excoriation, dermatillomania, or pathological skin picking, all of which in my opinion sound unnecessarily negative and even "crazy." It is also commonly called compulsive skin picking or chronic skin picking (CSP), which are more descriptive, less judgmental terms.

So it is called a disorder in psychological terms. But for our purposes, I don't believe we need to refer to it as a disorder with any special name in order to make it better, so I will call it simply skin picking. I even prefer to call it a habit rather than a disorder to avoid the implication that there is something *wrong with you*. And also because I believe, and have observed, that when people identify themselves as having a disorder, it tends to lead them to feel powerless, or to act as if they are powerless because they have a disorder. We are not powerless. We are infinitely changeable. If you don't have the power to change your own behavior, who does? Just because it's a learning process and you don't know how yet does not mean that you cannot.

"Excoriation (skin picking) disorder," is in the DSM-5 classified under the umbrella of obsessive-compulsive disorder (OCD), although there is some disagreement as to whether it is more like OCD or more like an impulse control disorder.

Most of the scientific research on skin picking is preliminary and of a descriptive nature; most of the articles published describe the behavior(s), survey the population to determine the numbers of people affected, and enumerate the co-morbidity with other disorders. There have been a few research articles concerning treatment, both with cognitive behavioral therapy (CBT) and with a few common pharmaceutical drugs, but all the treatment studies to date have been done on tiny sample sizes.

We may draw some parallels with trichotillomania, a more well-researched disorder in which individuals pull out their hair. Brain imaging of patients with trichotillomania and skin picking disorders shows that similar parts of the brain are affected in similar ways.[4] However, it does not currently appear that the two may be always treated identically. For example, the drug with the most evidence of effectiveness for skin picking has not proven effective for trichotillomania.[5]

That said, researchers have learned the following:

There is a huge range of behaviors that falls under the umbrella of skin picking. Common behaviors include popping pimples, squeezing healthy pores, scratching skin, peeling skin, using fingers or implements like tweezers to remove ingrown hairs and dig into skin. Once skin is removed or pus extracted, some skin pickers also smell, taste or even eat it. People also differ in the severity of the skin picking, the time spent doing it, the damage inflicted, and which body parts are affected. One research study estimates the number of skin picking sufferers in the U.S. at between 0.2%-1.4% of the population;[6] another found a 5.4_% prevalence.[7] Assuming a fairly conservative 1% means there would be about 3 million people suffering from skin picking in the United States alone. Many more women than men have a problem with skin picking – somewhere around 90% are women.[8] Skin picking often occurs together (comorbid) with other disorders and addictions, like anxiety, depression, bipolar, body dysmorphic disorder (BDD), obsessive-compulsive disorder (OCD), eating disorders, and substance abuse.[9]

The physical dangers include the serious risk of infection, chronic muscle tension and tightness from overuse of certain muscle groups, for example the forearm flexor muscles, or from contorting the body in order to pick. There have even been anecdotal reports of scoliosis being caused by hours spent picking in unhealthy bent positions.

Those who get skin infections as a result of picking are often in and out of hospitals and doctor's offices, and on antibiotics. The risks are continually increasing due to the emergence of dangerous multi-drug resistant infectious bacteria, which means antibiotics will not work against those bacteria.

The social and psychological costs are large too. Many skin pickers isolate themselves, not going out when they feel their skin looks bad. Internally they are conflicted and have low self-esteem from feeling they should be able to stop picking, yet not managing to do it, and also from feeling unattractive.

Scientific evaluation of treatment

Drugs for skin picking

The only drugs studied that have been shown to be effective in reducing skin picking are fluoxetine (Prozac™)[10] and, to a less certain degree, citalopram.[11] Fluoxetine has been shown to work in the short-term (up to ten weeks) but has not been studied beyond that. What I hear from my clients is that it helped some of them originally with their depression and anxiety and picking, but the effect then seemed to have leveled off or decreased in the long-term.

Topical drugs for the skin have not been shown to work for skin picking. Dermatologists have many skin picking patients, yet they have no idea what to do to get their patients to stop picking. "Stop picking" would typically be their best advice, yet it is unhelpful to the individual doing the picking. In addition, it makes the patient feel terrible because, chances are, he or she wants nothing more than to stop. Dermatologists may refer skin picking patients to psychiatrists who, beyond prescribing Prozac and trying other drugs that have not proven effective, usually don't know what to do either.

In my opinion, we cannot rely on drugs or the medical profession to help with our skin picking problem.

Psychological treatment

Cognitive behavioral therapy (CBT) has been shown, in small published studies, to be effective in reducing the amount of skin picking.[12] (And it has been demonstrated effective in larger studies with hair pulling.)[13] If you decide to see a psychologist for your skin picking, be sure they use CBT, and that they have experience using it for skin picking. The website of the Trichotillomania Learning Center (www.trich.org) has a list of practitioners that have been trained specifically to work with skin picking (and hair pulling). If none of these therapists are near you, you may decide to look for one with experience treating OCD or eating disorders, and share this book with them. (Eating disorders are similar in that, just as we cannot get away from our skin in the way an alcoholic can avoid alcohol, none of us can avoid food and stay healthy and alive.)

Some of the methods I will teach you in this book are methods that are part of CBT treatment for skin picking. They are simple and one does not need to be in psychological treatment to use them. However, simply using some elements of CBT is not the same as undergoing CBT treatment.

It is important to understand that there are other ways of reducing skin picking that have not (yet) been tested scientifically, but that are employed by professionals treating skin picking because they have found that these methods work with their patients and clients. Examples include hypnosis, relaxation techniques and dietary changes.

The story of my skin picking

My picking started gradually, although that's not the case with everyone. I remember doing it a little in my bedroom when I was in junior high or high school, just picking at the backs of my arms. They were bumpy, a condition I now know is called keratosis pilaris. It happens when the extra-fine hairs there block the pores. Although later I would squeeze around the pores with my fingernails, pushing out whatever filled them that was making them bumpy, when I was younger I did only what I had seen my father do many times – peel off layers of dry skin. (Although my father is a nervous sort of person, picking or biting his nails was something he did, yet not to the point where it was a big problem for him.) Peeling the dried skin on my arms was not as satisfying as peeling layers of recently sunburned skin, a phenomenon I had enjoyed when I was younger after visiting my grandparents in Florida. I had loved peeling off the thin transparent layer of skin a week or so after our sunny vacation. Sunburned skin came off so easily, sometimes in large pieces that made a crinkly noise, interesting visually and auditorially. Peeling around the bumps on my non-sunburned skin was also satisfying, but to a lesser degree.

I don't remember picking being a problem at all until I went to college. I think my other "addictions" kept me happy in high school - grade addiction and teacher approval addiction. I loved the high I got from getting good grades, and the attention that came with them from teachers and my fellow honors students. "What'd you get?" the boys would ask. I never asked first, because I didn't want to appear competitive and because I would feel bad for them if I asked first and did better than them. If they asked me first, that was a different story, and totally enjoyable. I also kept neat tallies of my grades each quarter in the inside cover of my notebooks so I could open them and look with satisfaction anytime I liked.

Perhaps partly because I never experienced a lack of highs from high school grade addiction, I never felt a strong need to pick until I hit college at SUNY Buffalo (UB), a large research university where I never spoke to a professor until my junior year, and where the work was much, much harder than it had been in high school. At UB, for the first time I began struggling in math and science classes. In high school I had won a special award for being the best science student in my grade, but by my sophomore year in college I had Cs in organic chemistry, a C- in physics, and a D in calculus 3. I had a hard time adjusting to the lack of structure of dorm life compared to the routine life in high school and at home. At home, I had much preferred doing math homework alone in my room to watching soap operas with my mother and sister. In college there were always people around to socialize with, especially when I was panicking over a physics problem and couldn't face it or the many other harder problems I would have to do to be ready for the tests. I hadn't developed the discipline to park myself in the library. I stayed up late and didn't sleep enough. It hardly mattered whether I slept through 8 a.m. physics class, because if I made it there I fell promptly asleep amongst the subset of the 400 students who actually made it there too.

English class stressed me out too, at first. Whereas in high school I had practically thought of myself as God's gift to science, I had considered English my big weakness, if only because others received better grades than me. In my all-or-nothing mind, I was either amazing at something or a failure. Senior year I opted not to challenge myself with AP English. At UB, I had a panic attack over the first English paper I had to write because I had never had to write that much in high school and couldn't imagine that I would be able to. The paper had to be 2-3 pages. The night before I started crying over it to my suite mate, who had gone to a really good public school (where she had actually been required to do writing assignments). She was compassionate enough to talk me down and through it. To my surprise I received a B+ and an encouraging comment from the grad student who was teaching the class. I was less anxious over English from then on and actually loosened up and enjoyed writing the four other 4-5 page papers we were assigned, for which I got A- and A's. All the assignments were based on the detective and horror fiction of our teacher's choice. "Interview with a Vampire" and Raymond Chandler stories were a welcome escape from the increasingly stressful science and math classes. For these, I had tremendous anxiety and plummeting confidence. So I began picking my skin more.

One afternoon during freshman year when my roommate was out, I was sitting on the top bunk peeling some dry-from-the-Buffalo-hard-water skin when I noticed a bump alongside my right nipple. I squeezed the skin around it, and to my surprise, a long string of white funneled out of the pore and just kept coming as I held my fingers there. Out and out and out it unfurled, twisting and twirling into a tiny pile of spaghetti. When I dug with my fingernails, more oozed out. I was horrified but fascinated. When no more came, I scooped up the pinky-tip sized pile onto my middle finger and rubbed the white cream between my thumb and middle fingers. I brought it up to my nose and smelled it. It smelled faintly cheesy. Seeing it and smelling it (and later, occasionally even hearing the pop of a pore when it released its contents) was exciting and deeply satisfying. Temporarily. It was like the first and best drug high that addicts are forever chasing. Almost immediately I wanted more— more of anything that relieved me from the anxiety of my daily life.

Squeezing intently with fingernails is bound to break the skin, and sometimes, at that point or soon afterwards, I began picking the backs of my arms to the point of damage. By sophomore year I had done damage; I know this because a boy I liked noticed the backs of my arms below my short sleeves.

"What happened to your arms?" he asked as he pushed up my sleeve and touched the bumps with their scabs. "Is it a rash?" I recoiled and hastily pulled the sleeve down, hiding the evidence again.

"No," I mumbled. I was never good at lying, even when spoon-fed the perfect lie. "It's just like that," I said quickly. I hoped he'd change the subject, which he did.

I tried to keep my activity and its ugly results hidden. Junior year when I moved out of the dorm and into a house, and later in graduate school, whenever I squeezed the pores of my face in the bathroom mirror, if I was likely to run into my roommates, I was careful to try not to do too much. Frequently in the evening I'd sneak out of the bathroom and make a beeline for my room, my face reddened and marked with fingernail indentations. By the next morning, my face always looked normal—not as good as it would look if I hadn't picked, but not too bad.

I don't know what people noticed, except for my mother. "Stop picking," she would admonish me, even when I wasn't doing what I considered the heavy work. I thought I was just running my fingers along my hairline, neck or face. "I'm not picking," I'd say, annoyed that she'd caught me doing *something*. Now I can see how she was unintentionally picking on *me* with those words, but that never occurred to me at the time.

One time my mother took me to a dermatologist who prescribed a hydrating cream for the backs of my arms. I'm pretty sure neither my mother nor I mentioned my picking, and the dermatologist either didn't notice the scabs or else didn't want to get into it. Judging from what I've heard from clients, no dermatologist has ever told them anything more helpful than "Don't pick," an entirely unhelpful and upsetting phrase, because we have all tried and tried so hard not to pick. I didn't use the cream for long. It smelled weird and made my arms sticky and ultimately more pickable, as the hard blockages in my pores were made soft and exuded more easily.

I tried to get help stopping when I was in my 20s and 30s, although not persistently. I tried psychotherapy and hypnosis each three times, and they never helped. I told the therapists picking was my major concern, but they thought it was just a symptom of other things that were wrong in my life, and that if I learned to handle stress in a healthy way the picking would go away. Each of the therapists was moderately, temporarily helpful in helping me deal with the rest of my life, but in terms of the picking, they never knew what to do. One therapist told me to wear thin cotton gloves at home so I couldn't pick, but that wasn't good enough; I just took them right off. Another one told me the picking would go away when I learned to soothe my inner child. That wasn't good enough either.

Even in my late twenties, I began to be aware of when I picked more and when I picked less. It is possible the first therapist encouraged me to do this, as it was around the same time that I saw her; I don't remember. After I went to the hip-hop dance class at my gym, I picked less. Indeed, I felt no urge to pick at all. When I was excited about something, even a phone conversation I'd just had, I picked more. When I had a cold or felt blue, I picked less, at first. But when I started to feel better, I picked more again, and even seemed to make up for the picking I'd missed. When I was upset, I picked more too. Although this kind of basic awareness is important, even with more awareness my picking continued to get worse throughout most of my thirties. I could afford to live alone, and so I did. But living alone, even with a cat, can be lonely. And there was nobody to stop me from engaging in any of my bad habits, from leaving dirty dishes in the sink to picking my skin.

The consequences of my actions accumulated and became more serious.

When I was a teenager, when many struggle with acne, the skin on my face was flawless, and in college it largely remained that way. By the time I was in my 30s, however, probably through a combination of stress and of constantly having my hands on my face and arms (and legs and chest and back - each year I found more parts of my body that I could pick), I either had acne or looked like I did. Even so, the spots healed well and left no lasting scars, until, when I was in my mid-thirties, they did. My nose and forehead always had blemishes I needed to cover with makeup, and picking the acne on my chin began to leave permanent dark spots that wouldn't go away.

I always felt the shame of having to wear sleeves and longer shorts to cover up the scabs. No tank tops for me. I had the continuous and ever-deepening feeling of failure because I was powerless to stop, yet I thought I should have the will power to be able to.

When I was 30, I moved across the country to become a biochemistry professor at a college in Los Angeles, and my life became more stressful. A couple of years after moving, I impulsively decided to leave and gave a year's notice with the thought of transitioning into a writing career. The school decided to push me out a year sooner and gave me a generous severance payment. By the second week of May, I had no place to go every day, and I had brought home boxes and boxes of science books, binders of class notes and files of journal articles that I wondered if I would ever need again. I felt disoriented and lost; if not a scientist, who was I? My anxiety escalated. Writing began to feel anxiety-provoking and soon ground to a halt. I was filled with doubts, and I was in total despair over the state of the skin all over my body and the fact that my picking was getting more out of control.

In July I learned Reiki, a form of energy healing that is calming, but is said to increase your energy vibration. This vibrational boost appeared to only increase my anxiety, except for the half-hour or so each day that I practiced the Reiki on myself. I was an anxious mess and picking plenty.

Desperate to stop, in August I found a therapist (my second try) and also saw my doctor and started taking Zoloft®, an anti-depressant. Although neither Zoloft nor any other medications have been shown in scientific studies to be hugely effective for skin picking, it seemed to reduce my anxiety for the few months I tolerated it. On it, I felt in a fog, which although generally undesirable, was a pleasant change from how I had been previously feeling. In September, I interviewed for a biotech job I was convinced I was going to get-the department head just had to find the money to hire me. So I waited, but felt calmer. I rode my bike on the beach and wrote a screenplay, because that's what you do in LA. When the job didn't materialize, instead of looking for more Ph.D. jobs around the country (jobs I knew I didn't want because I felt nauseous reading the job descriptions), I signed up for an intensive massage therapy course which began in January. I was always interested in bodily healing – Reiki, of course, which I took the second level of in November, but also yoga, chiropractic and physical therapy. Massage therapy was something you could learn inexpensively and quickly and then make some money at. I don't actually think it occurred to me in advance that I would have to expose my skin to the other students and teachers. I felt like I wanted to disappear the second day when we were practicing strokes on legs and the front of my upper legs were exposed in full view for people to see and touch. Nobody said anything - you're not supposed to comment on people's bodies, the teachers had taught us, not even to compliment. I just pretended that nobody noticed.

After a few short courses I got a job in a spa, three or four half-days a week, occasionally doing four or five massages in a row. Within a month, I injured my forearm muscles to the point that I couldn't work. In school we had learned good body-mechanics so we wouldn't get injured, and I know I used good mechanics. Any normal person doing that amount of massage in good form would have been all right. But my forearm flexor muscles were so severely tightened from years of picking they couldn't handle the stress of massage therapy, and I had to quit.

Lucky for me, though, being a teaching assistant in the massage therapy school made me want to teach again. One of the students said I was a good teacher, and that inspired me and made me think I could do it. I got another chance at teaching chemistry the following year in a great community college, and I went in with a renewed attitude. Although I regularly did the self-massage and exercises that one of the massage teachers taught me to do for my arms, for the next couple of years they hurt on and off when writing a lot on the board.

From the way I worked on my face, leaning over the bathroom sink so that I was an inch or two from the mirror, to the way I put my chin down and my elbows out so I could get at my chest, I also hurt my shoulders and neck. My jaw also tensed up, habitual tension I still carry around and am working on today.

Since the community college job was only half-time, when one of my students told me his friend was looking to hire a full-time chemistry teacher for a new school, I made the switch. The summer after my first year, I looked on Amazon for books that would help me stop picking and chose "The Complete Idiot's Guide to Breaking Bad Habits." I was serious about breaking my BIG bad habit. If there was a way to do it, I certainly had the will. I read it and actually did the exercises, a significant accomplishment since in the past I had read plenty of self-help books without doing the exercises.

The Guide never mentioned my particular bad habit, but it did teach me that all bad habits and addictions are generally about the same thing – trying to reduce our anxiety. We can break them when we 1) become aware of when we do them and 2) are able to replace them with a healthy way to reduce the anxiety.

The book instructed me to keep a "Bad Habit Log" before even trying to quit. Each time I picked, I had to write the time, the activity I was doing and how I was feeling. I learned, to my surprise, that frequently as I was about to pick, the thought that I was going to have to write it down afterwards deterred me enough to stop before I started. The first day I logged only four times, way less than usual. The second day I picked only twice.

That day I was so excited I felt like I could quit. For the first time, I really felt like I could do it.

Next, the Guide had me select a date for quitting. After day two of logging I felt so ready to quit I wanted to do it right away. A friend of mine had recently hosted a full moon beach bonfire party where she had us write down on slips of paper something we wanted to release. The full moon, she said, is a good time to release whatever is not serving you. (And the new moon is a time to bring in or start something new.) We had burned our papers in the bonfire to release whatever we had written there, and on the evening of my second day of logging, I looked out the window and saw that the moon appeared full. I looked online to check exactly, and learned indeed it was. I also discovered it was not an ordinary full moon, but a blue moon, the second full moon in a month, which only happens "once in a blue moon."

How fortuitous! I was convinced that the time was now to rid myself of this habit forever. I don't think the book told me to do a ritual, but I decided I would. No doubt, I had read of the benefits of ritual in another self-help book, but had not yet ever done one. Nevertheless, I walked out on my balcony and flipped the switch, lighting up the string of white Christmas lights atop the bamboo mat circling the balcony for privacy. I lit a stick of incense. Then I wrote a note: "Dear God, the universe, spirit guides, and any miscellaneous angels hanging around waiting for someone to ask for help: I no longer need this bad habit. Please assist me in releasing this habit, as I burn this note in the fire. Thank you. Amen. Sincerely, Annette M. Pasternak."

After signing, I lit the corner of the note with a match and dropped it into a vacant plant pot, where I watched it burn to ashes. Then I leaned back in my Adirondack chair and relaxed. I sat there comfortably, watching the incense burn and enjoying the warm summer night. I felt peaceful, an unfamiliar feeling. When the incense was gone, I went to bed.

The next morning I woke up with a dull but substantial headache. It wasn't like the headaches I got from stress and muscle tension, it was the same type of headache I had had when slowly tapering off that minimal dose of Zoloft I had taken for five months a few years before. It was a withdrawal headache. I realized I was going through real physical, biological withdrawal from the picking. All that squeezing of my skin, fingernails digging into the nerves, must have been releasing pain-reducing, stress-reducing chemicals like endorphins. For those first couple of days I couldn't concentrate on anything, and I felt like I was going out of my skin. Although I had started writing a book that summer, an as-yet unfinished memoir, I could not sit still to write. When I felt like I absolutely couldn't take it anymore, I left my apartment for a brisk ten-minute walk to pull weeds at The Learning Garden, a community/school garden where I sometimes volunteered. Digging and pulling up nutgrass for an hour gave me a sensory satisfaction similar to picking and got me through the antsy sensations. When I got back home and showered I felt calmer and didn't have the urge to pick.

I lasted two days without the teeniest pick. Then after that, a few times a day, the urge would sneak up on me and I'd do just an isolated fingernail squeeze. Just one, and then stop. It felt sharper, and even hurt, as if my habitual squeezing had kept down the number of pain receptors in my skin but they had repopulated almost overnight. Before I "quit," I could barely feel the skin under my nails. I felt a bit disappointed that I had lapsed, but I didn't want to feel bad. I wanted to feel successful, so I ignored my behavior and focused on feeling successful and proud and happy with how great my skin looked.

On day two, a friend of mine called just as I was feeling antsy and getting ready to go to the garden. I was also feeling proud of myself. I had never told her about the picking, and when I told her what I was up to, she said, "Ew!"—not the reaction I'd hoped for. I guess I was so excited about it I figured she would think it was really cool too. I pretended her disgust didn't bother me and went to the garden anyway, albeit with a little less enthusiasm.

Picking became more and more tempting as my pores filled up with all that good stuff that I was no longer allowed to squeeze out. Each squeeze now was more rewarding, more satisfying than they had been before I "quit." After a week or two, I got a facial, because 1) I knew pore extractions were part of the deal, and 2) I thought it would be a good reward. The Guide insisted that we reward ourselves for milestones. But I was underwhelmed with my reward. The goopy creams felt disgusting, and although the facialist did a little extracting, when I got home and looked in the mirror, my pores looked the same as they had before the facial, not emptied out anywhere near the way I liked to empty them.

My second year teaching high school started, and at first I was not too stressed. In September we had days off for the Jewish holidays and daylight time after school to ride my bicycle to the beach. There was also nothing to grade. But after a while the stress began to build. I don't remember exactly when it all happened, but by Halloween I was back to losing myself in front of the mirror.

I don't recall if I was completely back to where I had been before I "quit," but I began to feel hopeless, like a failure, even though I tried not to let myself feel that way. The Guide told me to expect to slip, and even offered a chapter on "getting back on the horse." The most important point was to return to keeping a log, so I did on and off over the next few years, but it didn't always help. I had never even seen this particular bad habit addressed anywhere, so I didn't know if it was breakable or not.

When I had the energy, I would try again to stop. Every year one of my New Year's resolutions was to stop picking my skin. Every year I failed. But some things gave me hope, like a radio interview I heard with David and Nic Sheff, a father and son who had each published memoirs about the son's addiction to crystal methamphetamine. Nic had gone to five different addiction treatment centers but at some point after each stay he had ended up back on the drug. He said that despite that fact, the rehab stays were never a waste of time. Every time he went he learned something, got something out of it. His enthusiasm and ultimate success gave me tremendous hope that I simply hadn't found all the pieces of the puzzle yet, but one day I might.

It would be about two more years before I found enough of the puzzle pieces to be able to at least see the picture, even if I was not able yet to complete the puzzle.

When I went away to a four-week yoga teacher training course, I imagined I could blast the picking addiction out of my system. I had been taking Sivananda yoga classes for a year, and could tell the effect it had on me at least for a few hours. I figured with the daily yoga, including asanas (the poses), pranayama (breathing exercises), meditation, chanting, healthy meals and not much opportunity for alone time, it could happen. At first I didn't pick, and didn't have much urge to, but after the first week or two, sometimes during my hour off in the afternoon, I could not resist a little picking, especially before bedtime. The high energy evening satsangs (meditation, chanting and usually a lecture or performance) ran until 9:30 or 10:00, and despite knowing the wake-up bell was at 5:30, it was hard to wind down and fall asleep.

At the end of the four weeks, I emerged happy, energetic, much more expressive, less held-back in my speech and less anxious. A changed person, but to some extent still one with a picking problem. It became clear to me that yoga helped but was not enough.

At the start of 2010, a half year after the yoga teacher training and when I realized I had backslid again, I thought to google skin picking and almost couldn't believe what I found. The OCD Center of Los Angeles, just fifteen minutes from my home, ran a Saturday therapy group for skin picking and hair pulling. Soon I attended my first meeting in the company of a handful of other women who had the same problem I did, plus another who pulled out her eyelashes.

That one was the charm. I attended for five months, and although I had not completely stopped picking, I was picking less over a longer period of time than ever before. I was also happy with my appearance; most of the time I could even wear a low-cut tank top and short shorts when I wanted to. Most importantly, I learned I could potentially stop. With persistence in the use of techniques that work, people do stop picking. I had seen it happen in the group (with people who picked worse than I ever did) and I had learned what I needed to do to control my picking. With a desire to have my Saturday afternoons free again, I left the group to continue the work on my own.

A few months after leaving the therapy group, I gave up sugar, and after a week or so, I was surprised to discover that I had no urge to pick anymore. Soon after that, I started adding a squirt of flax seed oil, a vegetarian source of omega-3 fatty acids, to my oatmeal each day. Within a few weeks the chronic joint pain I'd had for a year and a half disappeared. These personal experiments awakened me to the sometimes dramatic ways food affects us. When I met a holistic health coach at a dinner party, I knew instantly that that was the job I wanted to do. She told me about the great training program she had taken, and I signed up the next day.

During my health coach training, I learned more about food and how it and other aspects of life affect our health. In the training program I learned how to counsel and coach people to steadily implement positive change in their lives. Before the training, I had not even thought about specializing in helping people heal their skin picking, but the speakers encouraged us to consider who we would enjoy working with and what we uniquely had to offer. They suggested we might make those decisions based on our own health challenges. I realized that I was ideally suited to working with others with body-focused repetitive behaviors (BFRB's) like skin picking, and that this was work I would enjoy.

A few months before graduating from the training, I mapped out a program and began working with two clients who responded to my posts on an online skin picking forum. The program I developed did in fact help them both to greatly reduce their picking and to feel better about themselves overall. Slowly I added clients, learned more and continued to make my programs better and better, as well as more individualized. Although skin picking is typically the major concern of my clients, it is rarely their only health issue. Many clients have seemingly unrelated issues that *are* in fact related, symptoms of an unbalanced system that, along with addressing skin picking, we work to resolve together.

Today, I cannot honestly tell you that I never pick at my skin anymore. At times during writing this book even, my hand has absentmindedly gone to my scalp or my chest, and I've had to rein it back in. However, there is a freedom I feel. I know how to take care of myself, how to prevent little slip-ups from becoming a backslide into that canyon. I know that the freedom to finally stop exists in the moment, in every moment.

Those are the basics of how I got where I am: how I started picking, how I stopped, and how I came to help others learn to stop picking.

Now, you are going to learn how, too. Are you ready?

Section 2 - Breaking the Cycle

Getting in touch with your pros and cons

Breaking a deeply entrenched habit takes great awareness. It is so habitual that we may do it automatically. We have no hope against an automatic habit unless we 1) become more aware of when we are doing it, in what situations and in what states of mind we do it, and 2) employ specific strategies to give us a leg up on this sneaky habit. There is work involved and it takes great motivation to keep on top of it. To begin, it will be helpful to think about and write down all the pros and cons about picking and not picking. This will help clarify and bring to the surface your feelings and beliefs about picking and also about what it would be like to not be picking. On the next page or on a separate sheet of paper that you have divided into four quadrants, first write out:

1. Any pros of picking that you can think of. Does it feel good? Do you just like it? Does it give you an escape? Does it appear to help you relieve stress? Was it once a pro, helping you deal with something when you were younger, but now it doesn't feel like a pro?

2. Cons of picking. I'm sure you have many of these or you wouldn't be reading this book, attempting to stop. Write down as many as you can think of.

3. What are the pros of *not* picking? This one will likely be easy too, and a lot of it will just be the opposite of your cons. However, thinking of it in this way, you may come up with new things you hadn't thought of before.

4. What are the cons of *not* picking?

Fill out the sheet with everything you can think of, and then come back here and we'll discuss.

Pros of picking	Cons of picking

Pros of *not* picking	Cons of *not* picking

Okay, did you do the exercise? If not, I highly recommend you do it. It works if you work it. Reading can only get you so far. An action is worth a thousand words. Need I use any more clichés to get you to do it? One of my clients said it was the most helpful thing for her, because she is now more easily aware of her long-term goals in that moment she begins to go after her short-term gratification behavior.

Okay, so assuming you did your pros and cons exercise:

Did you discover anything? Did you get more in touch with something you may have felt semiconsciously but were not fully aware of until you articulated it? Did you have any cons of not picking listed in quadrant 4? When I lead people through this exercise on a coaching call, most people cannot think of one thing. They realize there is absolutely no reason not to stop, although they may be fearful of stopping. Any resistance they have is simply wanting the pleasure or stress-relief of the moment. Temporary pros versus lingering cons.

Some people say that one con of not picking may be that they would have no way of relieving stress. But that perceived "pro" - that our picking relieves stress, is misleading. We *think* our picking is relieving stress. Yes, it is temporarily relieving stress, but we will soon see that there is extra stress we have inadvertently put on ourselves by engaging in the obsessive-compulsive cycle of picking addiction. When we begin to break the cycle, we actually will feel more relaxed, not less.

However, it is a valid concern, that if we stop picking we will have no way of relieving stress. That's why an important part of a program to stop picking will be to learn other healthier ways of relieving stress. From learning to change our patterns of thinking so our thoughts become less stress-inducing, to physical and energetic methods of relaxation, to being sure the food we eat does not create stress, much of what you'll learn in this book will equip you to reduce stress naturally without picking.

Other clients say "never being able to get rid of a whitehead" or "having to go around with pimples that you aren't allowed to touch" are other cons. But that is assuming that picking is like an alcohol addiction, and must be abstained from 100%. That is not necessarily true. With advanced awareness we can choose whether it would be best to "groom" a spot or to leave it alone.

Notice the way you think and feel about the items in quadrant 3, the pros of not picking. Are you feeling sorry for yourself because you are not able to experience these pros, like being able to wear a bathing suit comfortably in summer, have the time to read, or to wake up, shower and be out the door with no makeup in twenty minutes? Are you wistful and sad about it? Or are you excited about experiencing them in the future? Your attitude makes a big difference, and with practice you can change your attitude. So get excited. Have faith. Know that is where you are heading. Look at those items in your "pros of not picking" list and start thinking, "Look at all I have to look forward to. I am on my way there." When you are clear about what you really want and focus on it, it is like a magnet pulling you on.

You may decide to make a pictorial representation of your pros of not picking, a vision board collage, in which you can cut out words and pictures from magazines that show you what you really want, and arrange and paste them in a way that appeals to you. Have fun making it, and then hang it somewhere and look at it often.

You can hang up your list of pros and cons, keep it by your bedside or fold it up and put it in your wallet. Look at the "pros of not picking" frequently as a reminder and motivator of why you are doing the work to stop picking. Daydream about the pros on your list. Make it all feel really real to you and you will be energetically drawn along the path to make it happen.

Introduction to the habit log

Have you ever started picking without even realizing it? Maybe you do it all the time. The habit log is a tool to help you cultivate greater awareness of your picking. Becoming more aware is essential, because only in a state of full awareness and presence are we able to make the choice to not pick. With a lack of awareness we are choosing picking by default, and it seems as if we have no control. It only becomes a choice when we are aware. It is still a difficult choice, not to pick. The instant gratification we get from picking is extremely hard to resist at first, but it is impossible if we are not fully aware in the moment.

In order to implement effective strategies for you to stop picking, you first need to know your picking habits and triggers. For example, where are you when you pick? What activity are you engaged in before or during? You will record these in the log, as well as any thoughts, emotions, or physical sensations you experience immediately before picking. You may not notice all three - thoughts, emotions and sensations - but do your best to tune in and record what you do have. Awareness increases with attention and practice. Finally, you will rate how strongly you feel the urge to pick, if you are aware of the strength of the urge. If not, rate the intensity of your picking. Do this with a number from one to ten, with one being "more like touching than picking" to ten being "uncontrollably the worst ever." At the beginning, keep the log for at least two weeks.

I cannot stress enough how important this exercise is, so please resist the tendency to think, "I know all these things, I'll just skip this." Do the exercise. You will learn from it. I know how horrifying it may seem to see it all down on paper. I know you may not want to face it. But it is essential. Today I would not work with any clients who do not complete the log. Earlier in my practice I had two clients who did not complete it, and guess what? They are the only clients I've had who have not made substantial progress in stopping picking. If you are not ready to do the work and keep account of your actions, you are not ready to stop picking.

Habit Log Worksheet

Date/time	Place	Activity	Thought	Feeling	Sensation	Time spent	Urge /intensity

What else the log will do for you

I promise that getting all the information about your picking down on paper, so you can see it as it is, will give you some insight that you did not have before. *Often, even the act of writing down your picking episodes begins to help you cut down.* You may be about to pick when you have the thought, "If I do this, I'm going to have to write it down," and the thought of having to go through the extra effort to log it is sometimes enough for you to stop before you start.

The process of writing down an episode immediately after you have it is a conscious act. Since writing is a conscious act that is tied to the time you spent picking right before, the likelihood of becoming more conscious, in the future, *as you do the picking* increases. You will be aware of yourself more frequently.

The log will also help you monitor your progress as you stop picking. Change is gradual, so sometimes without objective evidence it is difficult to see that we are making progress. For example, our critical eye may see that we still have blemishes, yet miss that they are not as bad as they used to be. When you keep a log you can add up the hours and minutes spent picking each week, and look back to see your progress, even by graphing it if you like. It can be very motivating to see you are making progress. Stopping picking is hard work, and for a while, it may not seem like it's paying off externally. Keeping track of the time spent picking is a way for you to focus on the positive and pay more attention to your progress than to how bad your skin may still look. Many of my clients consistently need to be reminded of their progress and to look at their accomplishments rather than focusing on their failures. Focusing on the positive brings in more positive.

Mini-log option

Although I strongly encourage the practice of keeping the full log in the beginning, and then as long as you find it helpful, you may find it gets tedious and time-consuming. You may even feel it keeps you overly focused on the picking beyond the point at which it is useful. If you need an alternative, a shorthand log can work for you. In this mini-log, all you need do is write down a number at the end of the day rating how much you picked, from 0-10, where 0 is no picking at all, and 10 the worst you have ever picked. A mini log will make sure you are staying on top of continuing your efforts to pick less, and will still allow you to notice your progress and setbacks. When you begin to use the strategies in this book, a mini-log can be useful for recording various other things, like the number of positive actions you took, the amount of sugar you ate, the degree of calm you felt overall, your overall mood, your energy level, sleep, etc. Mini-logs can be very powerful tools. I have had clients that have been very successful using only a mini-log after the first few weeks of the full log.

Another idea for when you are farther along the process is to use a phone app - I have used one called "habit maker, habit breaker" - and set a goal for how many picking-free days you can realistically shoot for each week. Then at the end of the day or the next morning you have the satisfaction of clicking the "pick-free day" button to record.

Summary:

The habit log is an important tool:

1. to increase your awareness of your picking, which will give you the power to reduce it.

2. to help you figure out the best strategies (in the next section) to help you stop picking.

3. to directly get you to reduce picking.

4. for monitoring your progress as you reduce picking.

"But I'm not *choosing* to pick. I can't help myself."
I understand that. We have no control over what is unconscious – it controls us. But we can work on increasing our consciousness, throwing light on the unconscious to make it conscious. When you are conscious, you can choose what is best. When you are unconscious, not present, you choose by *default*, you choose whatever is *easiest*. It is useful for us to think of it as a choice, to pick or not to pick, even though it is often a

very difficult choice, and a choice that is not even available to you when you are not fully conscious. I am not blaming or shaming you when you choose to pick; it often feels too hard to do otherwise. And nobody goes from zero awareness to complete awareness instantaneously. It's a slow process that takes practice. You are bound to slip, many times.

What to do with your log

After a week or two, examine your log. What can you learn from it? Are there certain places, activities, and emotional states that trigger your picking? For example, "I pick every night in the bathroom when I'm getting ready for bed," or "I pick when I am unsure what to do next. I feel anxious deciding and it makes me pick."

The following exercises will help you become more explicitly aware of the circumstances around your picking. After you do these exercises, making conclusions from your log, you will be ready to use the information in the following sections in which you'll identify which specific strategies to use to help you reduce your picking. Again, please don't simply read and think about them; get out a pen and write. Things become more firmly rooted in your brain and awareness when you write them down. Afterwards, you will have it all on paper in one place to refer to.

Part 1:

1. List the top five locations where you are most likely to pick.

2. Add the times you are most often in those locations.

3. List the activities or situations where you are most likely or tempted to pick.

4. List the top thoughts that trigger or precede picking.

5. List the top emotions immediately before picking.

6. List any physical sensations you noticed prior to picking.

7. Although I did not ask you to record this in your log, what are your top thoughts, emotions and sensations after picking?

Part 2:

Even for those of you who seem to pick whenever, wherever, if you look closely, you will discover that a picking episode does not suddenly appear out of nowhere (despite perhaps seeming that way). If you back up from the incidence of picking, you will notice that you have habits of action that lead you to the picking. In fact, there are typically several steps you habitually take that lead you to picking. Once you identify these "chains of events" it will become easier to interrupt the chain at its earlier events, sometimes with the assistance of the strategies in the next section. Interruption at earlier events is *far easier* than trying not to pick once you have already taken all the steps that habitually lead right up to picking. This is what Christina Pearson means in the book "Pearls: Meditations on Recovery from Skin Picking and Hair Pulling", when she says, "It's easier to stay out than get out." If you thought you only had one habit, this exercise will enlighten you to the various habits and habitual chains you have that lead to the one you think is causing all the trouble.

Here is an example of a habitual chain of events:

1. coming home after a hard day and feeling overstimulated (wound-up, antsy, etc.)

2. use the bathroom

3. wash hands

4. look in mirror

5. lean forward to get a closer look

6. look at and touch skin, feel around for a blocked pore to squeeze

7. use nails to squeeze pore

This is merely an example. Your chains will be unique to you, and you may have several different ones. It is important to become aware of what they are. Now, on a separate sheet of paper, list all your chains of events leading to picking, stepwise, as in the example above.

You did do it, didn't you? Great! You may have already noticed the top two habitual actions that lead to picking: 1) looking at your skin, and 2) touching your skin. In the next section you'll learn strategies to keep you from looking and touching your skin at those dangerous times, places and situations you have already identified.

The vicious cycle and the overall strategy to break it

Okay, here we go! The idea of this section is to give you concrete, simple and effective strategies to keep yourself from picking. Do not fool yourself into dismissing them, thinking these are temporary strategies that really can't help you in the long-term stopping of your behavior. Because by using the strategies, you are, in effect, retraining your brain. Our brains are incredibly plastic, meaning they are changeable, contrary to what scientists used to think.[14] The more you employ strategies that keep you from picking, the weaker the bad habit "grooves" in your brain will become.

When you delay or prevent picking your skin using any of these strategies, you may in the short-term feel the urge to pick more strongly than when you automatically gave in to it, simply because you are giving yourself the chance to feel it. But that won't last forever.

In order to understand what's going on here, we'll use the following model of skin picking. Your skin picking can be broken into two components: the urge to do it and the actual action of picking. Each feeds into the other, setting up a vicious cycle.

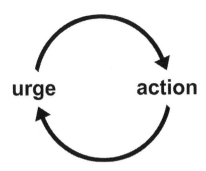

We feel the urge to pick, and so we respond to the urge by doing the action: picking. The action of picking gives us some short-term gratification, but after the feel-good effects wear off, we end up having the urge again. A long time ago, without realizing it, it was our responding to that anxious urge with action that actually created this vicious cycle. Immediately doing the behavior when we have the urge trains our brain to believe that the urge is intolerable and that the picking action is the best way to deal with it. Each time we act on the urge, we are feeding the cycle, ensuring that we will have the urge again. The action is fueling the cycle to continue.

But we want to break the cycle. Therefore, our approach will be to avoid doing the action using any means you find helpful. Retraining our brains in this way is difficult, but doable. The more and more frequently you can divert your attention to something else the better.

Sometimes the two parts of your habit can be so tightly coupled that you don't even realize that they are two separate things. You may be acting so automatically on the urge that you think there is only the action. That is why it is important to cultivate awareness, as we are doing in the habit log, when asked to consider the intensity of the urge, which is only possible to truly feel *before* the action.

You may think, when you feel the urge, that the longer you refrain from doing the action, the more intense the urge will become, and that it will never ease up. Luckily, this is not true! At some point the urge eases up and may even go away entirely. I remember how delighted one of my clients was the first time she experienced this. She had been in the midst of feeling and enduring the urge to pick without acting on it when suddenly she realized she had forgotten about it entirely and was thinking about something else.

At the beginning, if you are only able to prevent yourself from picking for a little while, think of it as a victory instead of a defeat. Because, initially it absolutely is. Any amount that you can loosen the coupling of the urge to the action is retraining your brain, making it easier for you to resist or delay picking the next time.

Blocking strategies

Now we're ready to get down to business. As you read these strategies, keep in mind the chains of events that you wrote down in the previous chapter. Remember that you want to use strategies as early on in the events chain as possible; otherwise you will find yourself unable to make the difficult choice to use a strategy rather than pick.

There are many strategies to help you break the automatic habit component of your skin picking. The idea is to make it more difficult, or even impossible, for you to do the action. It makes the process of stopping picking much easier. Using these strategies consistently becomes a good habit that you can use as long as you need them. Later, you can pick up again at any time if you feel you are slipping back into your old ways. Here are some useful "blockers:"

Cover your mirrors

If it's so automatic for you to lean in and start examining and picking your skin anytime you're around your mirrors, you may need to cover them. Go buy some pretty paper, something you wouldn't mind looking at for a while, and tape it up. One of my clients had a stand-alone full length mirror she would pick at. She covered it with fabric attached only at the top, so she could uncover the mirror when she needed to check out her outfit, but then cover it up immediately after. Now, of course, you may have to have some mirror to see how your hair looks, or to put on makeup, or see your outfit, but do your best to cover as much as you can. I covered the mirror in my bathroom completely. I also had mirrored sliding closet doors in my bedroom. I covered one of those with pretty paper, and habitually kept the other one behind it. When I needed a mirror, I would pull out the back mirror, and then push it back in when I was done with it.

There may be some awkward moments when you have visitors if your bathroom is also the guest bathroom. Once a friend of mine came over for the first time. He used the bathroom, then came out and asked me, "Is your roommate a vampire or something?"

Awkward, but worth it. It is **so** much easier not to pick your face if you don't even look at it. It felt like a great relief to me, to have that bathroom mirror covered.

"Help, I have roommates. Covering the bathroom mirror is **not** an option." True, it may not be an option for you to cover the bathroom mirror if you have roommates. Lucky for me, my roommate had her own bathroom. But if that's not the case for you, all is not lost.

Use dim lighting

Similar to the mirror idea that what you can't see, you won't pick, chances are what you can't see *well* you won't pick either. So make a habit of not turning the light on in the bathroom. When you need some light to see, either light a candle or use a flashlight. Keep these handy or you'll be tempted not to use them.

Other strategies for grooming and changing

Use a timer when you wash up, so you have to hurry along and can't take time to dawdle and likely pick. Same thing with the shower, if that is a picking hotspot for you. Estimate how long it would take you to shower in the absence of picking, set a timer and make it out by then. The same for changing clothes. Even if you don't use a timer, before you change, tell yourself you're just going to change your clothes, you're not going to look at or touch your skin.

If you pick while reading, using the computer, or watching television

Gloves may be your best friend. There are very thin gloves available, like the white waiter-style ones. Have several pairs so you can keep a pair near each place you typically need them. For best results, use them preventatively, *before* you need them. The more consistently you use any of these tools, the faster you will break the habit. I remember one woman in my therapy group stopped picking so quickly, simply because she got a pair of gloves and wore them all the time, everywhere. It was LA in the summer, and if I remember correctly, I think they were even those scratchy bath gloves, but she didn't care what people thought. After a few weeks, she stopped wearing them, and to my knowledge didn't re-start her picking.

If you pick while driving, you can buy and use driving gloves and make a habit of wearing them in the car.

If you find yourself ripping off your gloves to pick before you even realize you have done it, you may prefer finger bandages, like bandaids. They take more effort to put on, but they are so effective because they *take more effort to take off*. I personally loved those before bedtime. They made me feel secure. Once I had them on, I could enjoy reading in bed without ending up picking instead. I slept in them and took them off in the morning. You probably won't need to put them on every finger.

Another option is to cut your nails super-short or to use long fake nails. Truthfully, I was never able to cut my nails short enough to not be able to pick with them. Maybe it would slow it down for a day or two. But I've had clients for whom short nails was the most helpful thing ever. I'm also not the type to wear long fingernails, yet some of my clients have found it helpful to get acrylic nails or even the do-it-yourself cheap fake nails from the drugstore. I have also heard you can get gel or acrylic nails extra-thick, which are effective picking deterrents.

If you use tweezers or other implements to pick

Store them in a small cup of water in your freezer! Yes, they will be stuck in an ice cube, so they cannot be picked up and used on impulse when you have an urge to pick. Only when you deliberately thaw them out can you use them, which obviously you should only do for legitimate reasons, like pulling out hairs that are truly "out of place," not for picking.

Cover up

Another option if you pick large areas of your skin on different body parts is to make sure you have them covered up. Of course, the practicality of this suggestion varies depending on the climate and season; it's obviously easier in the winter to stay covered up. I had a big tendency to pick at my chest, so what worked really well for me was to wear a zippered fleece, zipped up all the way to my chin! Occasionally, I'd unzip and pick before I'd realize and have to quickly re-zip it. However, if I was wearing a regular-neck shirt it would have been much harder to stop.

3M makes large breathable bandages called Tegaderm* that stay on for several days. If there are particular body parts that you pick at badly, you can use those. I used them on my chest occasionally to break the habit of picking there. The only thing I didn't like about them is when I took dance classes and sweated. They would get itchy and hold in the sweat.

For how long do I have to employ these measures?

It depends. I kept my bathroom mirror covered for about a year. I had not stopped picking 100% and was worried it would be too much of a temptation and that I'd fall back into my old ways. I simply felt more secure that way. The mirrored closet door I kept covered the rest of the time I lived in that apartment, for probably two and a half years (partly because I thought it looked nicer than the mirrored door). I still keep gloves in my night table drawer, just in case, but I haven't used them in about a year.

Strategies to keep hands busy

Sometimes our hands really need to do something, and if we don't give them anything else to do, they will do their favorite habitual activity: picking at our skin. Whereas the last section was about "blocking" strategies, here we are looking at what could be called "redirecting" strategies; redirecting our "handsiness" to do other things. For example, I used to wear a hair elastic on my wrist, and play with it as needed. I typically would need to do something with my hands at times when my brain was working hard, like listening to a lecture or reading a book. That is typical and normal, that our hands need to move when we are learning. Carla Hannaford, Ph.D., a senior Brain Gym instructor and former biology professor, used to give her college students clay to play with during class, for this same reason.

When I was in graduate school and attended seminars on Wednesdays, there was another graduate student I noticed sitting towards the front with her elbows continually moving out from and into her sides, like a chicken. That was a mystery to me for a while, but it turned out she was knitting. She said it helped her pay attention.

A focused mind is a calm and happy mind, and these hand movements may be helping to create a focused state. It's not only the effect of the fingernails on our skin that is affecting us physiologically, but probably the repetitive motion of our hands as well.

Keeping our hands busy earlier in the day will sometimes satisfy their needs and we won't feel as great an urge later. One of my clients noticed this when she was working in a clothing store. The days she did a lot of hands-on at the clothing racks, hanging clothes on hangers, seemed to satisfy and calm her hands for hours afterwards. I experienced the same phenomenon with weeding in the garden.

Here are some ideas for keeping hands busy when they are agitated:

Weed a garden
Knit or crochet
Play with a rubber band
Play with a pen
Play a musical instrument
Fiddle with pipe cleaners
Doodle
Pop bubble wrap
Pet your dog or cat (my cat Cookie is well-loved)
Knead clay or putty
Play with a bracelet or spinner ring
Use commercial fiddle toys

Just as you keep gloves in your picking "hot spots," keep something around to occupy your hands in those same spots. You'll discover what works best for you, and you may change whether you prefer busy hands strategies or blocking strategies. The key is to persistently use some strategies and you will see great progress on your habit log (keep up those habit logs!).

Other Strategies

I always found I was most vulnerable to starting to pick at my skin when I didn't know what I was going to do next. It was a huge problem for me when I was unemployed or working part time. Not only did I have the anxiety that came from not enough work, and therefore not enough income, but mentally weighing the options of what to do the next several times a day made me feel anxious and stuck, and I would go right to the mirror to pick my face.

Indecision is also a big trigger for many of my clients. The solution is to schedule your time in advance. That is what I began doing. In the evening, I would plan out the following day in blocks of time, so I could wake up and follow my schedule. When all the decisions were already made the day before on paper, it was much less anxiety-provoking than deciding in-the-moment what to do next. It may take a little practice for you to set up a realistic schedule you can follow, but it's definitely worth doing.

Soon it will become a good habit, and we can all use more of those.

Another strategy is to set specific short-term goals for yourself and designate a specific reward for accomplishing each one. You just need to be thoughtful and creative, as well as realistic to make this work. Some people use stickers on a calendar for each day they make a daily goal, and then reward themselves with a movie or something enjoyable at the end of the week.

Remember to enjoy and celebrate your successes. There will be times when you slip up, but the key is, once it has happened, to not focus on your slip-up and berate yourself, but to get "back on the horse" and do your best to consistently use the blocking and redirecting strategies.

If you're having a hard time not beating yourself up, and you're still feeling completely ashamed and powerless about your picking, the next section is for you.

Section 3 - Reexamining and Transforming your Stress-Inducing Thoughts and Emotions

The next three sections of the book all deal with reducing stress. Picking is most frequently a response to, and the way we deal with, anxiety and stress, so stress reduction is key to getting our picking under control.

When you are stressed about something, whether it is work, school, getting along with your family members, or traffic, your body is reacting to your thoughts in the same way it did to survival threats in the olden days, when every now and then we had to contend with dangerous wild animals. Your body flips on the stress response, and the sympathetic nervous system turns on, readying you for "fight or flight." Your heart beats faster, your muscles tighten, blood flows away from certain areas (like the digestive system, and the higher thinking parts of our brain) that are unnecessary to respond to "danger" and flows towards areas that are needed immediately (like the skeletal muscles and brain stem). Stress hormones are triggered that rev up your entire system so you can optimally respond to the danger.

Our big problem is that the state of stress itself can become our habitual mode of living, if we experience it often enough, especially (but not exclusively) when we were younger. Our sympathetic nervous system is too often dominating, when what we need is to engage the parasympathetic nervous system. In contrast to the "revving" up of the sympathetic nervous system, the parasympathetic nervous system calms us down, with the result that we feel relaxed and peaceful. All healing takes place under parasympathetic conditions, and skin picking is certainly no exception. I'm sure you can relate to the "revved up" feeling that accompanies and triggers it.

In order to stop our dependence on picking, we need to shift our nervous system state from sympathetic (S) to parasympathetic (P). This is our strategy for most of the rest of the book.

S TO P to STOP picking

This section will help you with the mental/emotional stress you are creating with your own thought patterns. Thoughts can easily create stress in the physical body, as well as sabotage our success in this endeavor of stopping picking.

In Section 4, we'll work from the point of relieving stress at the level of the physical body itself, and also again at the mind, through techniques that come from Yoga and its sister science of healing, Ayurveda. The mind and the body are intimately connected, and it is important to know that 1) our thoughts influence our physical health, and 2) the converse is also true: a healthy, relaxed physical body has a positive effect on our mood and the emotional quality of our thoughts.

Section 5 is all about a huge effector of our physical health, and specifically our picking: food. The wrong food for your body can absolutely be a stress to your system and thus a big contributor to your picking.

Negative beliefs and skin picking

Your thoughts and the emotions they trigger have an incredible influence on your skin picking, not to mention how vastly they affect your entire life. In this section, we will first take a look at your emotional beliefs about yourself and your skin picking. Then I will teach you the basics of an amazingly powerful technique you can use to easily release yourself from these negative beliefs, as well as to reduce your skin picking urges. We will discuss the nature of thoughts and how many of yours are either false, or causing you pain, or both, and finally, how you can change your thinking to become empowered in your quest to stop picking.

In this exercise, you will be getting in touch with the deeply held negative beliefs you have about yourself and your skin picking. These are common beliefs among skin pickers – you are far from alone.

On a scale of 0-10, with 0 being "I don't agree at all" and 10 being "I agree completely," rate each statement honestly according to how you feel on an emotional level, rather than how you *think* you should feel or how much you intellectually believe the statement. For example, you may logically know you don't have to be perfect, but you may *feel* that you do:

_____ My self-esteem is related to how much I pick my skin.

_____ I am a loser because I pick my skin.

_____ I can't be happy until I quit picking my skin.

_____ No one will ever love me if my skin looks bad.

_____ I won't be successful until I can control this skin-picking.

_____ I have to be perfect.

_____ No matter what good I do in life, if I pick my skin, I will feel badly about myself.

_____ I am this skin picking.

_____ I am embarrassed of this skin picking.

_____ I am ashamed of this skin picking.

_____ I am embarrassed when people see my skin.

_____ I am afraid of what people think of me.

_____ No matter how hard I try, I can't stop this skin picking.

_____ I feel completely hopeless.

_____ I shouldn't lose control like that.

_____ I am angry at _____ that I have this habit. (Fill in the blank with whoever/whatever comes to mind.)

Please add any other negative beliefs you have about yourself and your skin picking:

All the beliefs that you have high numbers for are holding you back from healing. The negative emotions you have corresponding to these statements are energies that are out of balance in your body. When you release them, you will feel much better and have more personal power to apply to the process of positive change.

Emotional Freedom Technique
(Tapping)

We are going to use the Emotional Freedom Technique (EFT, also called meridian tapping) to release the emotions and reduce the stress associated with our negative beliefs. EFT was developed into its present form around 1990 by Gary Craig. It was distilled from aspects of Thought Field Therapy, a modality which grew out of Applied Kinesiology, which itself was based upon the acupuncture system of Traditional Chinese Medicine (TCM). EFT works remarkably quickly and successfully with otherwise stubborn psychological conditions such as phobias[15] and post-traumatic stress[16]. It is incredibly calming, which has been observed biochemically as reduced levels of cortisol.[17] EFT is simple and using it can not only make the process of stopping your skin picking easier, but can transform your life.

TCM describes a flow of energy in the body along subtle channels called meridians. Certain points along these meridians are sensitive to interacting with the environment – these are the acupuncture points, and they are measurable scientifically as points of lowered electrical resistance on the skin. The meridian energies interact with and nourish the bodies' organs, but energy is also more subtle than the physical body, more on the same wavelength as thoughts and emotions.

Emotions are energies that, ideally, flow freely through your body. You feel sad, so you cry. You get angry, so you yell or otherwise blow off steam, perhaps through exercise. Afterwards, you don't feel quite as sad or angry. But very often we don't express our emotions freely and so they get stuck, which can result in chronic depression or lingering resentment. Or they can be so stuck that they are not even felt as emotions, but are affecting the body, causing imbalance and physical illness over time.

Our emotions are triggered by thoughts. The negative belief statements you rated from 0 to 10 are thoughts that are linked with emotional states. For example, we may be ashamed of how our skin looks. When we read the corresponding statement, we emotionally access that state of shame, which is a negative emotion that has been stuck – we have been feeling it continually for a long time.

To release the negative emotional energy from your body, we simply tap lightly the ends of the acupuncture meridians seven or so times in sequence. Then, when we read the belief again and notice our reaction to it, we see it is not the same as how we felt even a minute earlier. The emotional intensity has gone down.

What follows a formal procedure for using the tapping points on a statement, such as one of the negative beliefs. However, you can also simply tap these points anytime you are experiencing strong negative emotions. For example, you can tap when you are feeling anxiety or intense urges to pick your skin. You can even tap after a picking session if you are feeling badly about yourself or regretful for picking. Do it when you are anxious and you may feel the urge to pick readily disappearing.

The procedure begins with a "set-up" statement that incorporates the negative belief into a format that reduces any unconscious resistance we may have to dropping it. For example, consciously, we want to stop picking. But there is an unconscious part of us that does not want to stop, and it resists and sabotages our efforts to stop. After we tap to the set-up statement, then we will tap repeatedly on the ends of several energy meridians, and the tapping will "unstick" the energy of the belief.

*A note before beginning: Although EFT is considered a very safe technique, if you suffer from serious disorders like severe depression, anxiety, or bipolar disorder, personality, psychotic or dissociative disorders, or if you have suffered from severe trauma, see a mental health professional who can use EFT with you. In these cases, or if you feel emotionally fragile, it is better to seek professional help rather than use this self-help procedure.

Figure courtesy of Rose Scheltema
http://eftpeace.abmp.com

EFT Instructions:

1) Develop a set-up phrase using one of the negative belief statements, according to this general set-up formula: "Even though I have this _____ I deeply and completely accept myself."

My coaching clients almost invariably have 9's or 10's for the shame and embarrassment statements, so I often combine those and lead them through tapping with the following statement, which we'll use as an example:

"Even though I have this shame and embarrassment that I pick at my skin, I deeply and completely accept myself."

Now repeatedly tap the "karate-chop" side of one of your hands with the fingers of your other hand as you repeat your set-up phrase three times.

2) Run through the points, tapping with medium pressure approximately seven times on each with your index and middle fingers as you repeat a short reminder phrase, such as "ashamed and embarrassed" once at each point.

3) After a couple of rounds through all the points, notice how you feel. Reread the statement and give it a new number. Is it less intense (and therefore a lower number) than before? Repeat the process (assuming the number has

not reduced to zero). When you do the repeat, adjust the set-up phrase to:

"Even though I **still have some of this remaining** ___, I deeply and completely accept myself."

In our example, this would be, "Even though I still have some of this shame and embarrassment at my skin picking, I deeply and completely accept myself."

And adjust the reminder phrase to, "remaining ___"
In our example, "**remaining** shame and embarrassment."

4) Repeat again if the number reduced further, but is still not at zero. Stop when the number is at zero or close. If other related thoughts pop into your head as you are doing this, you can tap with those too. Use your intuition. In other words, whatever comes to you while you're doing it probably came to you to help out. It is probably related.

If you are motivated, work on tapping for each of the negative beliefs you have identified, and see if you can bring each to feel like a 0.

Remember, anytime you are feeling badly, regardless of the cause or even when there feels like no cause, as with general anxiety, start tapping. When you are immersed in a present emotion, you don't need a set-up phrase. Just tap a few rounds and notice if you feel better. If you feel somewhat, but not completely, better, do more. It may take several rounds, but overall EFT is a fast-acting technique.

There are many variations on how EFT is done. The one described here is very simple but effective. I have often successfully used this simple format on myself and with my clients, and they also use it on their own to reduce anxiety and urges to pick, as well as to feel better *after* a picking session. One of my clients even does it with her elementary school-age children after they all get home from work and school. The kids think it's funny but it calms everybody down at a time that used to feel chaotic and stressful.

There are many ways to use EFT. These are just a few suggestions. If you feel that not all your negative emotions are being discharged, there are several possible reasons. You may need a slightly more complex, but still easy, method, or there may be other aspects of the problem you need to address. I have included EFT resources online in the appendix, including this video specifically on skin picking that you can tap along with.

Question your thoughts

We tend to believe our thoughts. After all, each of us has this voice in our head, thinking thoughts incessantly. Since our thoughts are always with us, it does not naturally occur to us to question whether or not they accurately represent reality. We assume our thoughts tell it like it is, but they are actually only a subjective reality that veils a deeper truth, that we are all beautiful and perfect souls. Besides the limitations and mortality of our physical bodies, the only other thing that makes us imperfect as human beings is our inability to see past the constant, typically negative thoughts of the mind.

Our identification with untrue negative beliefs causes us pain and holds us back from healing our skin picking condition. However, just as we are learning to become conscious of our picking habits and are working on modifying and reducing them, it can help us greatly to become more aware of our negative thought habits and train ourselves to change them.

Were you even aware that the thoughts you have are a choice? In a similar way that picking vs. not picking is a choice, so are the type of thoughts we have. With a little effort and practice, we can begin turning the tide of our thinking, choosing better thoughts whenever we are aware enough to do so.

How do we train ourselves to change a thought? Since awareness must necessarily precede change, just like with our picking habits, we need to become aware of the ways in which we think, especially those ways which are negative. Luckily, we can identify certain kinds of negative thinking that are common to most of us, and that are likely to be habitual in your mind. Later in the chapter, I have classified common habitual negative thoughts in several categories. As you read, notice which are thought patterns that you frequently have.

As we become aware of a negative thought we are having, it is valuable to question whether it is true. (Chances are good, though, that if it fits in a category I list below, it is probably a negative and false thought.) The inquiry method I demonstrate in the next paragraph is adapted from the work of Byron Katie, and for more practice I highly recommend her book, "Loving What Is."

When you notice yourself thinking a negative thought, ask yourself, "Is this true?" and "Can I be absolutely sure this is true?" Usually, you cannot have objective evidence proving that it's true. For example, if you find yourself thinking you are a loser, does ALL evidence point to you being a loser? I bet your dog doesn't think you're a loser. Maybe your dog is right! Are there no other explanations for your situation other than you being a loser? Next, when you understand that you cannot be absolutely sure the thought is true, think about what happens to you when you believe that thought. Does it make you feel bad? Without the thought, would you feel happier? So, can you see how it might help if you simply drop that thought? Does feeling bad really serve any purpose?

Realize that, with awareness of a negative thought, it is only a choice to think differently. It may feel unnatural to you at first, but see how it feels to replace the thought with its opposite. In our example, "I am a winner." Perhaps you don't believe the new thought, but remember how bad the thought "I am a loser" makes you feel. Wouldn't you feel and act differently in life if you thought "I am a winner" instead? Can you imagine how it might make you feel more able, with more energy available for good habits, like those you are learning in this book to stop picking? Who do you think will do less picking, the "you" who entertains thoughts of being a loser, versus the "you" who dismisses those thoughts, and who is beginning to think she is a winner instead?

You are so much more than your skin picking habit. And yet, what manifests in your life is what you think about. Besides the time you spend picking your skin, how much time do you waste thinking about it? Feeling badly and thinking negative thoughts about yourself because you do it? Think to yourself right now: what might I be able to accomplish with all that time? What might I be able to do with more productive or positive thoughts? How might I feel?

So practice this simple yogic technique of replacing a negative thought with a positive one. I know a man who succeeded in using this technique as a child when he was afraid there was a monster under the bed. He started thinking about Santa Claus instead, and felt better. Become aware of your thoughts, and cultivate positivity. You are not your thoughts, so treat them lightly. Don't be overly disturbed by negative ones - you don't have to believe them. Just be aware and choose a more positive thought, even if it feels fake or if you don't believe it (at first).

Years ago I had a friend who, when she heard me saying something bad about myself, would say, "Hey! Don't talk about my friend that way." Be a good friend to yourself. Catch yourself when you have negative thoughts or say bad things to yourself. Catch yourself and replace the thought with the opposite. Even if you don't believe it yet, you're opening the door to believing it.

Positive thoughts make our bodies feel good – nice and relaxed. Negative thoughts change our body posture, our body chemistry. Thoughts of gloom and doom make us feel depressed. Thoughts of anger and frustration make us tense. If you tend to pick more in states of depression or anxiety, can you see how changing your thoughts over time can make a big impact in decreasing your picking?

Okay, as promised, here are some typical negative thought habits to look out for:

All or nothing thinking

One important thought habit to recognize is "all or nothing" (also known as "black and white") thinking. This often manifests in the life of a skin picker once we've begun a picking session. You didn't intend to, but now you're Britney Spears and it's all, "Oops, I did it again." BEWARE OF YOUR NEXT THOUGHT. Is it "Oh well, I might as well keep going now" or some other thought that leads you to keep picking because you've "failed?" Perhaps you think, "What's the use," "Today is a total loss," or "Now that I've started picking, I can't stop." Are those thoughts really true?

No, they are all false beliefs that you are accepting as true, simply because they are your habitual automatic thoughts. Just because you've started picking doesn't mean you have to keep going. Yes, it *is* harder to pull yourself away once you've started than it would have been to simply not look in the mirror in the first place, and the part of you that enjoys it doesn't want to stop. But that doesn't mean you *can't* stop - at your first awareness of what you're doing, if possible. Think about it, question the situation: Isn't twenty minutes of picking objectively better than two hours? Even though you are still picking, 1) you're doing less damage than you would do in two hours, 2) you have more time to do other things (six times as much time in this example), and 3) you're training your brain to stop picking once you've started, so it will, over time, become easier to do so. We can even add 4) you're learning what activities work for you to do next instead of picking – activities that are sufficiently distracting and satisfying so that you don't go straight back to picking.

If you think about this whole picking thing in an all-or-nothing way, your thoughts are definitely getting you in trouble. If you are stuck in this kind of thinking, there is no way to win, unless you never, *ever* pick at your skin. Well, I have news for you: most of the population picks at their skin. Okay, not to the degree that you do, but if you accept that you do pick your skin and allow yourself to be okay even though you pick, you are going to have much greater power to choose not to pick in any given moment, leading you to reduced picking over time, and eventually maybe no picking at all. Imagine a future in which you slip up and pick a little only occasionally as you continue to learn to deal with your stress. You can look at that future positively or negatively. If you pick a lot now and hate the way your skin looks, why not choose to feel good about a near future of *less* picking, rather than bad because in that future you're still picking? Actually, why not simply feel great now, knowing you are on the road to reducing your picking.

If you have in your mind that you're only okay if you do zero picking, you are setting yourself up to *never* feel okay.

Permission giving

Once you have a handle on all or nothing thinking, another thought demon might sneak in: the kind of thought that gives you permission to pick. Is "just this one" a common phrase you tell yourself? Or, "I've had a bad day; I deserve this." Or how about, "I've been really good lately, so I deserve this." Or "I can do this because I feel really in control now, so I'll just squeeze a couple of pores lightly and not do any damage." Stop for a minute and think of your common versions of this story. What thoughts do you have that lead to picking via permission giving? Write them down now! Be more conscious of them, and don't fall for them! Be wary.

Question your feelings

Sometimes we feel a certain way and automatically believe that, because we feel it, it must be true. Objectively, though, just because you *feel* something does not mean it's true. For example, perhaps you feel your partner doesn't love you anymore. This is your perception and may not have anything to do with the reality. Perhaps he (or she) is busy and stressed from work, or has been frustrated because in his mind he has tried to make you happy. If you are not fully aware of what is going on, you may wrongly assume his recent lack of romance is evidence that he doesn't love you. Another example: maybe you feel stupid. I felt stupid for most of the time I was in graduate school. Was I really stupid? No, I was learning a difficult process (research) in a difficult subject (biophysical chemistry), and I had an overactive negative mind that responded automatically to any setback with anxiety and negative thoughts, the primary ones being, "I'm stupid" or "I'm not smart enough." If you pay close attention, you can notice that emotional feelings actually come as a response to a thought rather than on their own. If I had held my thoughts up to inquiry, reasoning whether they were objectively true, I probably would not have believed them. *But I did not reason, I just kept thinking them.* The effect of thinking them was to make me feel badly. If I had done the inquiry, beyond asking whether they were true, if I had asked what it was costing me to think that way, I might have seen the pain my thinking caused, the unhappiness and drama and doubt in myself, and how it was all distracting me from what I really wanted to accomplish.

So, again, beyond questioning whether a thought is sure to be true, if it is not 100% certain that it is a true thought, ask yourself what it does to you when you think it. Does it make you unhappy? Then, regardless whether it may be true or not, why think it?

Need or want?

Another thought or feeling you likely have that goes unquestioned is the feeling that you need to pick your skin. You may feel that anytime you have a bump or pimple or scab or flake you *have* to do something about it, you have to pick at it to make it right, to fix it, or simply because it's there, or you may believe you *have* to pick because you have such a strong urge to do it, because of either a physical sensation or negative emotion you don't want to face. Question that emotional thought that tells you that you need to pick. Is it really true that you *need* to? What would happen if someone came into the room at the moment you "need" to pick? Would you still do it? If the answer is "no," doesn't that suggest that maybe you don't really *need* to pick, but you just really, really want to and *feel* like you need to?

Please know that I am not saying the feeling or the urge is not strong, and I am not saying it is easy to resist it, or that it is your fault when you find yourself unable to resist it. I am merely saying it is theoretically possible to choose not to pick. Believing you absolutely must pick makes you a powerless victim, and ignores the truth that you have a choice between two options: picking and not picking. Even though one option is difficult, and the other easy because it is habitual, if you want to make progress, you need to understand that it *is* a choice. To begin with, you will not be able to consistently make the difficult choice. It takes awareness and the willingness to forgo temporary immediate satisfaction in favor of your long-term goal. These qualities take practice to develop. We get better bit by bit rather than all at once. There is no sense looking at "no picking" as the only acceptable state, and "picking" as failure. Discipline is a quality that must be cultivated; it grows over time with practice. Same with forgoing the immediate gratification of picking. Look at stepwise progress as success. Expect during your progress that some picking is inevitable, and not a reason to feel like a failure. Think of it as information telling you what you need to do better next time. And remember, if you are reading this book in sequence, some of the most powerful techniques to help you stop picking are yet to come, so please don't be discouraged!

Mind reading and taking things personally

Never assume you know what others are thinking. Let's say someone looks at you and then quickly looks away. You may automatically jump to the conclusion that, "She's grossed out by my skin." How does that thought make you feel? Lousy, right? And you don't even know if it's true. There are many possible reasons she looked away, including that she may be exceedingly shy, possibly even as self-conscious as you. (Who knows? At the same moment, she may be saying to herself, "Why can't I make eye contact? I'm such a loser.") Unless they tell you, you cannot know for sure what people are thinking, even judging by their facial expressions. Back when I interviewed for a job as a professor, I had to give a talk to students and faculty about my research. As I started the talk, I was nervous. My voice was monotonous and flat, because I had so much fear and lack of confidence about my performance. I looked out at the audience and my eyes went straight to a student who was slouched in her seat and giving me the most disgusted look. Because of my negative beliefs about myself and my performance, I naturally assumed she was disgusted by my talk and how badly it stank. That assumption zapped every last drop of confidence I had left. However, I managed to get through the talk anyway, and I even got the job. Two years later, when the same student was in my classes and research lab, I mentioned how I had been surprised she wanted to do research with me, since she seemed so far from impressed during my job talk. "Oh, I remember that day," she said. "I had food poisoning. It was so awful, I felt like I was going to throw up the whole time." If I had known not to read people's minds or take things personally, I wouldn't have been so affected by her nauseated expression. How much better off would you be if you made it a policy to 1) never make assumptions about other people's thoughts, and 2) never take their actions personally?

Don't "should" all over yourself

If you find yourself thinking, "I shouldn't be doing this" all the time, it implies guilt on your part. You are constantly making yourself wrong, or bad, or "less than" when you think (or say) "should" thoughts. The same goes for any thoughts of anger towards yourself and your behavior. These are negative thoughts without which you would feel much better. So train yourself to catch them. Self-acceptance is a necessary step to healing. "Should" is resisting what *is*. The thought that, "I shouldn't be picking" is not accepting yourself as you are in the moment. Paradoxically, the tighter you hold onto believing that you shouldn't be picking, the less able you are to stop. In order to change, we need to accept ourselves where we are. That thought that you shouldn't be picking your skin? It is untrue, simply because you *are* picking your skin. When we stop resisting reality, we release tremendous energy that was tied up, energy that becomes immediately available to help us make positive change.

Even a thought of, "I should stop picking," implies that you won't. Can you see how the thought, "I could stop picking" is more positive and more likely to actually get you to choose to stop?

Over-focusing, magnifying, and assuming others think the way we do

A skin picker is obsessed with skin, a hair puller with hair, a nail biter with nails, a compulsive dieter with weight, etc. We all notice the particular body part with which we are obsessed, much more so than any other. We skin pickers are overly focused, not only on our own skin, but also on everybody else's. We believe our own particular distortions, so if we notice this woman's skin is good and that woman's is bad, we may tend to envy the first woman and judge the second, as we harshly judge ourselves. Then we assume others are judging us horribly too, because of our skin. The truth is, everyone is more preoccupied with their own lives and insecurities than with everyone else's, so if you are thinking, "That person must be disgusted that my face looks so gross," chances are good that it's not true. And what is it costing you to believe it? Probably your happiness and mental well-being, as it likely makes you feel bad to believe it.

It is very possible that because you focus so much on how badly your skin looks, you actually think your skin looks much worse than it actually does. If you hide out and miss social activities or even work because you think your skin looks terrible, it's likely that, although it may not look very good, it probably looks better than you think. Whenever possible, fight against your world closing in on yourself - resist your impulse to hide out whenever your skin looks bad.

Keep in mind that "perfect" skin does not exist any more than a perfect person exists. We all have flaws, inside and out.

While we are talking about assumptions, a related thought to question is the kind that assumes we have it so much harder than anyone else. Perhaps you project that the woman with the "perfect" skin has the "perfect" life, but chances are that is not true. Nobody's skin is perfect, nobody's life is perfect, and you have no idea what that woman is dealing with in her own life. Everybody has their own challenges, no matter how outwardly perfect their lives appear to an outside observer. Envying someone else and feeling sorry for yourself are useless thoughts. (And how do they make you feel?) So do your best to dismiss them.

Positive thoughts attract positive, and vice versa. You can never jump up the rungs of a ladder; you have to go step by step. Please let go of the attachment to being perfectly healed, with perfect skin and no picking NOW. You can hold that as an ideal, where you'd like to be someday, but accept that that is not where you are now, and be okay with that. Do your best to enjoy the process of discovering how to make human-size improvements in yourself and your picking. Remember the tortoise and the hare story? It is the truth; persistence wins. Get rid of the thought that you should be there NOW, that you should not have this affliction. It is a useless thought, resisting "what is." It is negative and only holds you back from where you want to be.

Help, I can't seem to control my thoughts.

"Help, I know I'm having negative thoughts, but I can't seem to help it – they are circling in my head and I can't get away from them." There are times when you will feel overwhelmed and out of control in this way, as sometimes negative thoughts pile up on each other so fast you have no chance to examine and encounter them individually. In times like these you need a distraction to break the negative spiral. Get out of the house. My favorite feel-better outing has been riding my bicycle to the beach. Other good possibilities: go for a walk, meet a friend, exercise, take a yoga class, see a funny or uplifting movie, go for a nature hike, read or browse the Internet at a café so you're around other people, rather than alone at home.

The idea is to distract yourself in a healthy way that is not going to create or exacerbate any other addictions or tendencies. If you feel you absolutely cannot get out of the house, do some exercise, write, pray. Put on some music and dance. Think of one thing you are grateful for. Thought of one? Think of two more. Watch a funny TV show. Just be careful you don't watch too much television or waste too much time on the internet because of the passivity and addictive quality of both.

Homework: Be on guard and notice the negative thoughts you have over the next several days - about your behavior, your body, yourself, and any assumptions you make about others and what they are thinking. What more positive thoughts can you replace these with? You may want to keep a journal on this topic for the next couple of weeks. It will help keep the topic on your mind so you become more aware of your thought habits and change them.

Further reading on the topic:

- "Loving What Is" by Byron Katie. Or you can read about how to do "The Work" online.
- "Change Your Brain, Change Your Life" by Daniel Amen
- "The Four Agreements" by Don Miguel Ruiz
- "Overcoming the Rating Game" by Paul A. Hauck

Focus on the positive

Let's do a quick exercise. Look around you, scanning to notice everything red in the room you are in. Did you do it? Good. Now close your eyes and recall everything blue. Open your eyes and check. How much blue did you miss? How much more red could you remember, simply because that is what I asked you to focus on?

Life is like that. What we pay attention to creates our experience. In addition, what we pay attention to grows. When you plant seeds and then water and tend to them, you can grow a plant, even a tree that bears fruit for you in the future. Similarly, we are continually planting seeds in our minds, then "feeding and watering" them with our attention. Eventually we reap the results. What thoughts have you been feeding and watering with your attention and repetition? Thoughts have energy and a gravitational pull – they attract similar thoughts, as well as lead us to similar actions and like-minded individuals. Every action we do had its motivating force in a thought. This is the meaning of karma, a fundamental truth found in eastern religions and yoga philosophy, and also in the Bible: "Whatsoever a man soweth, that shall he also reap." Of course, karma includes women too. It is universal.

If you are continually focusing on your picking, and your negative thoughts about yourself and your picking, you are reinforcing the inertia of those kinds of thoughts. They become more and more powerful. So how can we focus on what we want, rather than on what we don't want?

1) The Positive Log

Most of my coaching clients hit road bumps of discouragement along the way, even when they were making progress that to *me* was evident. Their discouragement came from the (natural) tendency to focus on what they haven't yet achieved. They were still over-focused on the picking they were doing, or on their scars, even though they were continually learning and doing less picking. This is when it is valuable to start keeping a *positive log*.

In a positive log, which you can do at the end of each day, you write down all the good-for-you actions that you took that day, actions that you know from reading this book will lead to reduced skin picking. The key is to focus on the positive actions that you have control over, rather than the picking behavior. I also recommend keeping the 0-10 rating of amount of picking alongside it, so you can identify how your positive actions relate to the amount of picking.

For example, one evening's log might include:

1) started the day with a breathing exercise (see Section 4)

2) brought a healthy lunch to work

3) did tapping after I picked and felt discouraged

When you write down the positive actions you are taking that you have learned will lead to decreased picking, you will get a feeling of satisfaction and positive momentum that you *are* moving toward your goals, whether they be freedom from picking, clear skin, or whatever your particular goals are.

2) A Gratitude Practice

Gratitude and appreciation are powerful positive thought seeds that can grow and uplift us, and give us energy for whatever we want to accomplish in life, including, of course, stopping our compulsive picking. Appreciate the beauty of nature, your material surroundings, and other people. You may want to make a gratitude list or daily journal – each morning or evening, write three things for which you are grateful. Even if (especially if) your day sucked. Even on the worst of days there is something positive to focus on. And don't get upset thinking how pathetic it is that these small things are the best part of your day. That is a needless negative thought! Simply appreciate the small things. Acts of acknowledging even small things with gratitude are seeds you are planting to grow something positive in your future. Have faith and trust that they will bear fruit.

The worst thing you can do, in my opinion, is curse that you have this skin picking problem. From a larger perspective that you may not be able to see yet, either having the problem or learning to heal from it (or maybe both) is teaching you important lessons you are here in this lifetime to learn. It can be a blessing, and it is wonderful when you are able to see it that way. At the very least, please be open to seeing that any amount of time you spend cursing your picking and wishing you didn't have it is wasted time, and wasted energy.

Focus on what you want rather than on what you don't want. Focus on the way you want to feel. Imagine how you will feel, relaxed and happy and with clear skin. This kind of visualization, of states unfamiliar to you, will be much easier and come naturally as a result of the calming techniques in the next section.

Section 4 - Calming, Focusing and Grounding

The techniques you learned in Section 2 can help you break the habit of your skin picking, but they are usually not enough by themselves. This is because your picking probably evolved as a way to deal with stress, and your life may not have gotten any less stressful. When you are feeling amped up, antsy, agitated, or otherwise stressed or overstimulated, if you don't know techniques you can use to quickly calm down, which will be suitable *replacements* for the picking, you will resort to your number one choice for dealing with feeling overstimulated – yes, picking, the very thing you'd like to be free of.

Scientists are not sure what causes compulsive skin picking, but some suspect a glitch in sensory processing. At times of high sensory input, we are regulating ourselves, calming ourselves down by the picking process. For many of us, the urge to pick increases during the day, and becomes worse in the evening. If this is true for you, this sensory-overload must be addressed. This section explains how, using specific sense therapies, breathing exercises and meditation.

This section has many concepts from Yoga and Ayurveda because I personally have found them so helpful in thinking about life and its meaning in general, and about what is going on in our bodies and minds specifically regarding this skin picking problem. The techniques of both are so transformative. So please join me as I geek out on all this Sanskrit!

Sense therapies from Ayurveda

The ancient Indian medical science of Ayurveda (a "sister science" of Yoga) is still used today not only in India, but in the United States and many other countries around the world. From Ayurveda we learn ways to calm the senses, ground, and nurture ourselves, which will all help reduce our need to pick our skin. Ayurveda uses a model in which we are comprised of five elements. In order of grossest to subtlest, the five elements are: earth, water, fire, air and ether (space). The elements combine to make up what are called the three doshas, or constitutional types. Earth and water combine to make kapha, which is grounded and nurturing. Air and ether combine to make vata, which is light and quick (think of the speed of thoughts). Fire alone is the pitta dosha, which is fiery and energetic. We each have a predominant dosha, or we may be a combination of doshas. There are questionnaires available online if you would like to determine your doshic constitution.

We may also have a dosha imbalance. The predominant imbalance in our society is in the vata dosha. Most of us are "vata aggravated" because the pace of modern life is so fast. Too much anxious thought and worry, scattered thoughts, not enough focus (attention deficit everywhere) and everything is fast, fast, fast, especially in the information age with computers and cell phones constantly with us. Imbalanced vata energy causes addictions. It seems especially relevant to compulsive skin picking when we consider the individual elements again. Each element has associated with it one of the five senses, a receptive (sense) organ, and an expressive organ of action. The sense of the air element (comprising the vata dosha) is touch, the sense organ is the skin, and the organ of action of the air element is the hands. So, naturally, an inbalance in the air element can lead to skin picking, which involves exactly the two organs involved, the hands and the skin.

There are sense therapies in Ayurveda to help calm the air element, and they are healthy and natural ways to decrease your need for skin picking. One such therapy that has been shown to reduce stress[18] is abhyanga, the practice of massage or self-massage with warm oil. To do abhyanga, put some sesame or almond oil in a small closed container and heat the container in a pot of water on the stove until the oil is warm but not too hot. Then stand on an old towel and begin the massage at your feet. You can do long strokes on the muscles and circles around the joint areas. Work your way up, and you can even massage your scalp and oil your hair. If you are comfortable, sit quietly for five minutes to allow the oil to soak into your skin, close your eyes and relax. Breathe deep slow breaths. Use a paper towel to blot excess oil, then take a shower with soap and shampoo. If you do abhyanga regularly, the towel you stand and sit on will eventually become too oily to launder. Just use it for abhyanga for a while and then throw it away.

If it is too much of a picking trigger for you right now to be naked and touching your skin, I recommend the (non-Ayurvedic) practice of "squeezies," which you can do fully clothed. Starting from one ankle (or foot if you like), wrap both hands around the ankle and squeeze with firm pressure for about seven seconds. Then move your hands up to the next part of the leg and repeat. Keep traveling up the leg. When you get to the top, squeeze the hip and buttock. Then repeat with the other leg. Then do your arms one by one (of course you will only have one arm to use for squeezing), starting at the hand or wrist and working your way up to the shoulder and above to the trapezius muscle between the shoulders and neck. You can do gentle squeezies on the side of the neck, and even squeeze the sides of your torso.

As you do any of these practices in this section, notice how you feel before, and notice after. Do you feel calmer, more grounded?

Other good ways to calm the air element using the sense of touch are to pet and hug your animal friends, hug other humans, and go outside and feel the sunshine on your skin, or the ground beneath your feet.

As vata also comprises the ether element, we can focus on balancing ether as well. The sense associated with the ether element is hearing, the sense organ is the ear, and the expressive organ is the vocal chords. Loud music is unbalancing, as is verbal abuse and even some silent speech such as negative thinking. Many skin pickers have had the experience of being picked on, even by family members, and our picking actions are simply an internalization of being picked on. We may even have been "shut down" at the level of expressing our true selves. We also tend to be perfectionists, and our self-talk is often brutal. The work we do in changing our negative thoughts and replacing them with positive ones (Section 3) is balancing the ether element. Mantra meditation, the silent repetition of a positive thought or name of God, is another therapy for balancing the ether element, as is singing, listening to uplifting music and allowing time for silence.

As the action associated with air is using the hands and that for ether is expression of word or thought, journal writing or writing affirmations can also be helpful.

Vata is calmed and nurtured by kapha. Because we are likely to be deficient in kapha, using sense therapies of the kapha dosha helps as well. Kapha is a combination of water and earth elements; taking baths uses the water element, engaging the sense of touch in another nurturing way. You can bring in the earth element too, with the sense of smell in the form of aromatherapy. Adding a few drops of a relaxing essential oil, like lavender, into the bath makes it an even more soothing and grounding experience. Vata is cold and dry; a hot bath goes a long way towards calming it down. Hot baths in the evening greatly relaxed me and decreased my skin picking urges.

Grounding calms vata. Exercise outside that connects us with the earth is grounding, and standing or walking barefoot on the ground is especially grounding and healthy. Many aches and pains disappear simply from spending time barefoot on the ground.[19]

Pranayama

A key to stopping picking for many of my coaching clients is using a simple yogic breathing technique that I will teach you in this chapter. Pranayama, loosely translated from Sanskrit as "breath control," is an ancient yogic practice to calm and steady the mind. Used strategically it can be one of our most important tools to stop picking. Pranayama helps to increase our awareness, improves our mood and overall energy level, yet quickly and powerfully calms us when we are overstimulated. Skin pickers tend to have nervous minds, and are easily overloaded sensorially. Not only is the practice of pranayama one of the best ways of calming ourselves when we are agitated and feeling strong urges to pick, it is also excellent as a preventative measure to do regularly once or twice per day. It has been shown in scientific studies to be effective for anxiety and even for acute panic attacks[20] and post-traumatic stress disorder (PTSD)[21]. It is a healthy simple practice with such profound effects that I wish it would be taught to children in elementary school.

The manner in which we breathe reflects our state of mind. When we are stressed, we breathe shallow quick breaths; when we are relaxed, we breathe long slow deep breaths. Conversely, the manner in which we breathe also greatly affects our state of mind. So in order to relax the mind (and body), all that is necessary is to slow and deepen the breath.[22] Purposely breathing slowly and deeply is a simple example of pranayama.

In yoga, pranayama is practiced in a cross-legged position, but you can do it in a chair if you are more comfortable. You can even do it standing, if needed, for example, in a crowded subway. The wonderful thing about this technique is that you can do it anywhere to calm down, and (unlike the EFT tapping) nobody will even notice. If you are sitting, sit tall, but comfortably.

The basic methods of pranayama are done by breathing only through the nose, for both the inhale and exhale. The first key to deep breathing in general is to start with an exhale in which you squeeze out as much air as possible; to do this you contract your abdomen in towards your back, squeezing the abdominal muscles in. The next inhale will automatically be deeper. As you inhale, the abdominal expands outward from your body. After the abdomen expands you can expand the ribcage as well to bring in even more breath. Abdominal breathing engages the parasympathetic nervous system, allowing us to get out of a "fight or flight" stress response and relax.

Before going on to the exercise below, be sure you have mastered the simple deep abdominal breathing. Babies naturally breathe as above, but through stress or the desire to hide what we may consider a fat stomach, many of us have acquired a habit of shallow breathing into our chest only, and as we breath in, our abdomen moves *inward* as the chest moves up and out, and as we exhale our abdomen puffs outward. This pattern is backwards from the natural abdominal breathing explained above. If you are breathing in this reverse manner habitually, even working to change that habit should have a tremendous effect on your energy level and state of mind.

When you are comfortable with deep abdominal breathing (which may be right away or you may want to practice a few rounds a day for a week or so), continue with the following exercise – a counted deep slow breathing with a breath retention and an exhalation that is twice as long as the inhalation.

Remember S TO P to STOP picking? This ultra-relaxing type of breathing I'm about to explain is supercharged to take you from S to P and calm you down FAST:

1) Abdominal expansion – When you puff your belly out on the inhale, proprioceptor nerve cells in the diaphragm, the muscle you use to breathe deeply, send a signal to the brain to relax.

2) Breath retention – Holding the breath for a few seconds signals the brain to shift us from S to P to slow down bodily functions like the heart beat and muscle tension, thus relaxing us.

3) Longer exhales – Slow exhales further engage P to relax us.[23] We also breathe only through the nose, which also forces the breath to be slower and thus, more relaxing.

Before you begin, notice how your body feels and your state of mental agitation or calm. To begin the exercise (after first squeezing all the air out of the lungs), inhale for a count of four seconds, then retain the breath for a count of eight, and finally exhale for a count of eight. Repeat. To begin with, do four repetitions. Notice how you feel afterwards. Remarkably calmer? And in only a minute or so! Also, notice the strength of any urges you felt to pick. Have they lessened?

Sign up on my newsletter list
(http://www.stopskinpickingcoach.com/free-gift) to instantly
receive a free video in which I lead you through this exercise
(plus you get a free report and more).

If you can discipline yourself to do it, beginning and/or ending the day with this exercise can go a long way, with the calm alertness you feel spilling over into the rest of the day or night. You can work your way up from four rounds to seven, eight or even ten rounds. If you tend to get antsy in the evening, doing the breathing right before dinner might be a good practice for you. Or you can practice it whenever you have a spare minute, sitting at a stoplight, waiting in line, or whenever.

Another great way to use this breathing is when you are having urges to pick, and are in danger of picking. Clasp your hands in your lap (or sit on them if you need to) and make yourself breathe instead. When you are done, if you still feel the urge to pick, you may need to breathe some more. Commonly, my clients tell me something like "The urge went away, but came back a half hour later." Well, that was a victory! But you know what? You might need to do it again, or do more than four rounds. If you, like many of us, are resistant to "wasting" more time breathing, think of how much time you waste picking, and know that any time invested in calming techniques like this breathing exercise is time well spent.

I know you may be resistant to doing the breathing exercises regularly or especially when you feel like picking. It takes a lot of motivation, and when your body is in that tense state of being about to pick, it is hard to sit still and simply breathe. Yet when you do it, it is extremely effective.

Often the hardest part when you are in that "about to pick" state is remembering to use the tools that help you. Here is the strategy for that: Whenever you remember, whether it is before you would pick, in the middle of picking, or just after a session of picking, do the breathing exercise. Have the intention that you are going to couple breathing and picking together, and you will begin to remember it more easily. The ideal, of course, is to do the exercise before any picking happens, so it will calm you down and prevent you from picking, at least for a while. However, in order to get you to this point, do it *after* any picking too. Your mind will begin to associate picking with the breathing exercise, and before you know it you will be remembering to breathe *before* you pick, and eventually it will become a good habit you will use all the time. Eventually you will not need to pick, and you will not need to use the breathing exercise as often, although you may still choose to do it as a healthy, calming daily practice.

Meditation

Ultimately, the most powerful aid to successfully stopping any addictive behavior over the long term is a regular practice of meditation. Meditation calms the physical body and the mind and reduces the anxiety or stress response that is a major cause of our urges to pick. Meditation reduces our negative thoughts, and increases our awareness of the nature of our thought process. It is a practice of focusing the mind. A focused mind is analogous to a calm lake. Whereas a turbulent lake with many waves is opaque, a still lake is clear and we can see through the water to the bottom. When we calm our thought waves by focusing the mind, we "see" what's underneath, which according to yogic philosophy is pure consciousness, complete bliss and infinite pure love. Also infinite potential, since in accessing this state, anything is possible. We may also think of it as God, our ability to connect with God, or our soul. The ability to focus your mind gives joy and clarity that has the capacity to uplift every aspect of your life. A focused mind lifts depression and brings joy. Studies have shown meditation reduces both depression and anxiety[24] and has a healing effect on many diseases.[25] What's encouraging is they have shown it works even when it feels like it's not working, when you think you're not particularly good at it. And meditation has been proven scientifically to have benefits even with as little as ten minutes a day.

No doubt you have occasionally experienced the satisfaction of a focused mind. Think of something or some time when you were totally absorbed in an activity. It is sometimes called a state of "flow," where you lose the concept of time and are not thinking of anything else. Athletes or artists often get into this focused state. It is a highly enjoyable experience simply because the mind is focused. For some of us, picking or pulling puts us in a flow-like state, and we feel we are in a trance. That is why it is so addictive; it accesses a focused and, in a way, joyful state, but with negative consequences. Many addictive behaviors have in common the temporary focusing of the mind – shopping and television are two powerful modern day addictive behaviors. The problem with depending on these behaviors is that they are external, and the mind in their absence is unhappy. Meditation is so powerful because the focus is *internally* directed; you are developing the ability to focus and therefore to feel relaxation and joy regardless of external conditions. Have you heard the phrase, "happy for no reason?" Happy for no reason is the state of an advanced meditator.

With a focused mind comes complete awareness. Only with a focused mind can we see beyond the mind, through the thought waves to the bottom of the pond: our awareness. We are not the mind; when we slow the mind through practicing meditation, we find that we can *observe* the mind. Because we *are* that awareness. It is our true nature. When we are in touch with total awareness, we have the power to make choices, and we make the best choices. We are aware of an urge to pick, but we are also completely conscious, able to feel the urge yet do nothing but simply experience it without reaction. We make the choice not to pick, and with total awareness and calm, the urge will pass away.

Picking is similar to eating without awareness. For example, in a movie theater your attention is elsewhere, but you keep going for the crunch of the popcorn until it's all gone. You want more and more because you are not experiencing eating the popcorn with full awareness of its taste and crunch, etc. If you were doing nothing but focusing on eating the popcorn, you would likely desire less of it. Similarly, with more consciousness, we would not pick as much.

Meditation may not feel easy, and it is not instant. It takes time to develop the focus of the mind. It takes practice. But I can promise you, if you practice daily (or even better, twice daily) it will be worth every minute invested. Deepak Chopra, M.D. says of the addiction programs at his Chopra Center, "In our decades of experience working with people attempting to free themselves from addictions, we have found meditation to be the most powerful tool to change negative patterns. In fact we have never witnessed a person relapse when they are meditating regularly."[26] Of course, a relapse is easier for a skin picker, simply because our skin is always more accessible than a drink is to a recovering alcoholic who has cleared their home of alcohol. I would never say that practicing meditation guarantees no picking. Nevertheless, meditation works regardless of the addiction or negative habit.

There are many methods of meditation practice. My experience is in mantra meditation, the same method taught in the addiction programs developed by Deepak Chopra, M.D. at the Chopra Center, also in the Yoga of Recovery program of Durga Leela, and in Transcendental Meditation* (TM), a popular system on which there has been a large amount of scientific research demonstrating positive physical and mental health benefits. Most psychotherapists who teach meditation teach mindfulness meditation, which has been an active area of research as well, also showing many benefits. If you're interested in that route, you can take a mindfulness course online especially for BFRBs with Christina Pearson, the founding director of the Trichotillomania Learning Center. In addition, two psychological treatments that are considered promising for BFRBs like skin picking have a lot of similarity to meditation practice: Acceptance and Commitment Therapy (ACT)[27] in which patients are taught to observe urges without responding to them, and Dialectical Behavior Therapy (DBT)[28] which teaches mindfulness and distress tolerance.

It does not matter which method of meditation you use; it appears that the benefits are the same. The important thing is to choose one method and stick with it. The analogy for this concept is to "dig one well." If you are digging a well, and keep moving from place to place to make shallow holes here and there, you are not going to get down deep enough to find the water. Similarly, it takes the continual practice of one kind of meditation to get the deepening required to find and dwell in that peaceful "place." Since I practice mantra meditation, I will teach you that.

The word *mantra* in Sanskrit literally means "protects the mind." Repeating the mantra mentally interrupts the habitual patterns of our thoughts. If we really pay attention, we will notice that most of our thoughts are negative or simply not useful. A focused mind has the power to create more of what we want in our lives.

A fine mantra to use is "Om." In Sanskrit, "Om" is said to be the primordial sound from which all other sounds, and in fact all creation, comes. As the Bible says, "In the beginning there was the Word, and the Word was with God, and the Word was God." The Bible may not say what the word was, but the Vedas (the ancient source of Yoga, Ayurveda and more) say it was "Om." All the major religions have a tradition of meditation, so you can do some research to find a mantra that suits you. If you are uncomfortable using any mantra, simply follow the procedure below with no mantra. Focusing on your breath alone will work too.

As always, with any procedures you try, notice how you feel before, and then notice again after. Noticing is an important part of the learning process, and when you notice the benefits you are more likely to do the activity again and again.

How to practice meditation:

1. Find a comfortable way to sit with your back straight, either on a chair or cross-legged on a cushion. If you use a chair, be sure your feet are comfortably on the ground. If you use a cushion, sit at the edge, allowing the knees to lie lower than the hips. Doing so helps keep the back straight. Clasp your hands on your lap, fingers relaxed.

2. Always give your mind a set time. Use the timer on your phone or invest in a kitchen timer, so you do not have to open your eyes to look at the clock. Start with ten minutes. Gradually, as you begin to enjoy your meditation practice, you may choose to increase the amount of time sitting.

3. Take a few deep breaths and consciously do your best to relax each part of your body. There will of necessity be some muscle tension necessary to keep you upright, but release excess tension. For example, no tension is needed in your face.

4. Allow your breath to calm down until it is almost imperceptible. Bring your attention to your heart at the center of your chest. If you like, you can imagine feeling the breath entering and leaving your body at this point. Repeat your chosen mantra with each breath. If it is a short one like "om," repeat once on the inhale and once on the exhale. Do your best to keep your physical body

still during meditation practice. Keeping yourself from fidgeting will help your impulse control in general; the benefits of practicing stillness will carry over into resisting your urges to pick.

5. You will doubtless have many thoughts coming to mind. Do not let this disturb you. It is the nature of the mind to be very difficult to focus and "still." Any time you discover that your mind has been running away with thoughts again, simply redirect it to focus on the mantra and the feeling at the center of your chest. Do not be frustrated by the seemingly constant stream of thoughts; that will only agitate the mind further. Just be persistent, continually and gently, time and time again, redirecting your awareness to the focal point in the chest and to the mantra.

By the way, I have often found it helpful to think about practicing not picking in a similar way to practicing meditation. It's almost like the reverse process. In meditation, when you notice thoughts, you gently bring your attention back to the mantra and focal point. Time and time again, with no reaction or frustration. With picking, when you notice you are picking, or simply looking at your skin or touching it in a way that leads to picking, you gently stop picking, remove your hands or look away. As often as necessary, with no reaction or frustration. As you learn to stop picking, you will find yourself picking many times. It is most effective to simply redirect yourself to not picking without unnecessary self-chastising thoughts or frustration. Just simply redirect, over and over again as needed. Just like a reverse meditation.

The most important thing is consistency. Doing a little meditation practice each and every day is more beneficial in the long-term than doing an occasional marathon session. There will be plenty of times you don't feel like meditating. In the past five and a half years since I started a daily meditation practice first thing in the morning, there have been many, many days I have gotten up and not wanted to sit down and meditate. But I know it's the best habit I've ever made, and I certainly don't want to fall out of the habit, so I sit down and do it. And I always feel much better, usually almost as soon as I sit down.

We don't really break habits. We make new ones to replace the old. When we make healthy new habits like meditation, we grow and our lives improve. It may appear difficult and you may have all kinds of inner resistance, but when you commit to doing it every day, it becomes easy. The resistance is all in our mind. When we don't give our mind the option to vacillate and debate every day whether we're going to do something, like meditate or not, there's no question, and it is easy. I may have the thought fifty mornings in a row that I don't feel like meditating, but since I have unquestionably committed to doing the practice, it's not an option in my mind to skip it, and it's easy.

When I took the meditation course at the Sivananda Yoga Vedanta Center in Los Angeles, the first thing the teacher, Vidya Chaitanya, said was "You better have a damn good reason for doing it," or you just won't do it. Nobody told me meditation would help my skin picking, but that was the reason in my mind unquestionably (even though it could also be said that the rest of my life wasn't working too well at the time). Either I intuitively knew it would help or I just had faith. I thought, "Ohhh, yeah, I have a damn good reason," and committed to it. You can too. Do you have a good enough reason? Then figure out a regular time to do it, find your space, inform anyone who needs to stay out of your way, and just do it.

Exercise, rest, and other lifestyle factors

You may have already noticed conditions that make you "ripe for the picking." Insufficient sleep is one of the most universal. Just as you are more susceptible to catching colds if you have not been getting enough sleep, you are also susceptible to doing more picking when you haven't had a good night's sleep, or especially if sleep is a chronic problem for you. If you are in a vicious cycle of not getting enough sleep at night followed by the need to drink a lot of caffeine during the day, your system is going to feel very stressed and off balance, and you will tend to pick more.

If at all possible, do your best to get to sleep regularly by 10:00 or the latest 11:00 PM. Avoid watching television or using the computer in the hour or two before you go to sleep. Especially if you tend to pick at night in bed, simply turn off the light when you get into bed rather than read. If you feel wired, try listening to a self-hypnosis or relaxation recording. If falling asleep is a chronic challenge, you may decide to investigate the use of 5-HTP before bedtime (see the supplements chapter in Section 5). Getting some sunlight (or a sunlight lamp) during the day can be helpful too, as it will trigger the body to convert serotonin into melatonin, the substance that brings on sleep. (In the body, 5-HTP converts directly to serotonin, which can then be transformed into melatonin.) At night, avoid bright light for a couple of hours before bedtime. You can replace regular lights with amber colored ones, and that will help your body get ready for sleep.

If you haven't been getting enough sleep *because* you're picking at night, doing the work in other chapters to reduce your picking is really going to have a wonderful effect on your life when you are finally free to get more sleep.

Alcoholics Anonymous has a reminder acronym HALT, that is totally applicable to skin picking as well. HALT urges us not to get too **h**ungry, **a**ngry, **l**onely or **t**ired, because in those conditions we are most vulnerable to a setback. Have you noticed these as triggers for yourself? My clients have noticed that "tired" especially is a big trigger. That is probably because our conscious mind is less in control, and our unconscious desires take over.

There are other ways of slowing down your hyper brainwaves. You can listen to hypnosis or relaxation recordings in the evenings before sleep (or even to help you fall asleep if that is a problem for you). Or you can try seeing someone for neurofeedback sessions. Neurofeedback measures and helps you train your brainwaves, so it can help you shift from the more high frequency, anxiety producing waves to the slower more relaxed waves.

Exercise is another extremely important factor regarding stopping picking. Have you noticed you pick less or can ease your urges to pick by exercising? If not, try it! Vigorous exercise is especially helpful in dispersing excess scattered energy and thus calming you and relieving the urge to pick. (At the very least, you are unlikely to pick *while* exercising.) Exercise is also a mood lifter that has been shown scientifically to be as effective as anti-depressant pills.[29] Exercising just before a typical pick time for you can be especially effective in helping you stop. If you are too out of shape for vigorous exercise, a walk outside can help greatly instead. Yoga is also helpful and can give you good practice staying calm, mindful and breathing deeply while experiencing a challenge.

Other lifestyle factors to consider are the use of cigarettes, alcohol and other drugs, and the company you keep. Alcohol can increase picking. Because of the stimulant nature of nicotine, it's possible that cigarettes may have an effect as well. Some of my clients have noticed decreased picking after smoking marijuana, but that is not a healthy way to regulate yourself and reduce the picking. It will cause you more problems over time, so I do not advise using it.

Stimulants often cause skin picking to start, not to mention worsen a picking problem that already exists. Besides crystal methamphetamine, which causes skin scratching and picking, there are also instances of stimulant medications for attention deficit disorder (ADD), like Adderall and Ritalin, causing skin picking.[30] If you take ADD medication and found that your skin picking problem either began or worsened at the same time, consult with your doctor to find another medication or see a Brain Gym* Instructor/Consultant for movement-based resolution of ADD.

Who we spend time with influences our well-being. Although, as children, we don't have much choice about who we live with and how stable/healthy/loving they are, when we are grown up we do. Some people are uplifting, some drag us down or drain us. We tend to spend the bulk of our time with people who are similar to us in terms of our mental state of positivity vs negativity. But we can change our internal state, for example, by changing our thoughts or meditating. Then we find that we begin to want to avoid other peoples' negativity more, and we attract more positive people. Sometimes it seems we are tested. We may need to make a conscious choice to release negative people before the more positive ones come into our lives. Trust that it will happen.

For many of us, picking is a source of pleasure and comfort, and one we have relied upon for a long time. We all crave pleasure and comfort, and these are deep needs. I believe the teachings of yoga, that our *true* need is to realize that we are already infinite love and peace and bliss, not a body with its problems, and a mind with its issues. To know that nothing can truly disturb us, that we are one with God or the Universe or your higher Self, however you like to look at it. While that is our one true need, it can feel like a slow process getting there.

In the meantime, it is important to find pleasure and comfort in ways that are truly healthy, and not likely to be addictive. What do you really love to do? Dance, draw, paint, run, sing, laugh, walk on the beach, hike in the woods, etc. Whatever it is, am I right that you don't do it often enough? Why not? I always really enjoyed fashion magazines and light fiction books, yet for years I withheld those small pleasures from myself because I considered them frivolous and a waste of time, and I "should" be reading science journals. Why was I being so mean to myself? Why withhold something I enjoy from myself? Life is short. Make it a priority to treat yourself better. These days I have a subscription to "In Style" and look forward to it each month. If you are like me and tend to withhold "guilty pleasures," I advise you to regularly indulge in some, so you don't feel deprived. As you cut down on the picking, and especially if you change your diet, you may notice feeling somewhat deprived. Your success depends on you not feeling this way, because otherwise you will unquestionably go to your #1 go-to for comfort.

My dance classes are my playtime. I have fun when I dance; I leave my life somewhere else and just enjoy. I make them a priority. Life for most of us is serious enough. Make playtime a priority, whatever that means to you. Whatever gives you joy is going to put you more in touch with your soul and make you feel better.

Especially if you are a mother, you give to your children and are probably not nearly as good at taking care of yourself. Children are the top priority, but you need TLC too. It is not sustainable to continually feed yourself poorly, deprive yourself of sleep, relaxation, exercise and doing things *you* enjoy. You will be unhappy and that will serve no one.

Emotional Stress Release and other energy techniques

An excellent technique I teach often is the Emotional Stress Release points (ESR) from Touch for Health. This is another technique to use when you are worried or stressed. Simply touch your fingers to your forehead, or lay a hand across it, and hold for a few minutes. That's how mothers naturally soothe their children, isn't it? And what do you do when you realize you forgot something important? "Oh no!" you say as you slap your hand to your forehead. That's because it works. The ESR points are neurovascular points. That means they are thought to work by bringing blood flow to the front of the brain, our most highly evolved area of the brain where we make choices and reasoned decisions. We may even feel a connection to God (some people pray with their fingertips on their forehead). It gets us out of the stress response in which we are "stuck" in the back of our brains, in its less evolved, more "lizard-like" functioning.

I lead people through this technique whenever I teach free introductions to Brain Gym® (a modality that uses movements to make learning anything easier). You can use it for stress in the moment, or you can use it to feel better about upcoming situations you are worried about. I

154

usually ask people to think about either an upcoming event they are stressed about or a person they have been having conflict with. Then I turn on some soothing music and lead them as we hold our ESR points. When I ask people to think about the situation again after even holding for just three minutes, most people feel a freedom about it, and more relaxed. As one woman said, holding the points "took the edge off." The situation may be the same, but they feel better about it.

There are loads of other simple movements, postures and hand positions that affect and can work to balance the energy in our body and mind. Yoga and Tai Chi are two movement-based systems that work with energy and result in greater physical and mental health. Scientific studies have shown that yoga is effective for more than 75 health conditions, including OCD. Simply practicing savasana (corpse pose) - lying face up with arms (palms face up) and legs away from the body - can be transformative and deeply relaxing and renewing.[31]

Joan Kaylor, in her Secrets of Pulling and Picking app, demonstrates another exercise from the Touch for Health/Brain Gym repertoire that helps you tolerate and reduce skin picking urges.

Section 5 - Food and Supplements

During my recovery process, I remember one of my fiercest picking sessions happened the morning after attending a fancy party for a friend's 40th birthday. That night I overate rich food, including sugary birthday cake, plus I drank champagne *and* wine, when I would rarely drink either. I stayed up late and then woke up early, partly from habit and partly from the after-effect of the wine. Then I had coffee with breakfast to wake up more. That morning I broke down and picked my skin uncontrollably. Mornings weren't usually even one of my "danger times."

Does what you eat affect your picking? I would have to say, absolutely yes. And the statement, "You are what you eat" is not a meaningless cliché. We are all individuals. Experimenting to find a healthy diet for you is well worth the effort. There is no such thing as a "one size fits all" healthy diet, and your dietary requirements will even change at different points during your lifetime. However, there are some general aspects of diet to consider that will help you greatly reduce your picking. We're going to divide these considerations into two parts. In the first part, "Are you getting too much?" we will discuss foods and food issues that contribute to skin picking. In the second, "Are you getting enough?" we will cover foods and dietary habits to incorporate that will help you minimize your skin picking.

Food: Are you getting too much of these foods?

Too much...

Sugar

I consider this one of the most important parts of this book. I cannot overemphasize how bad sugar is, not only for your general health, in that it is a huge contributor to the general inflammation that underlies almost every degenerative disease we know,[32] but also in its role in skin picking. If you are like my clients and me, you will almost certainly notice a substantial decrease in your urges to pick upon eliminating sugar from your diet. I was shocked to notice what a tremendous effect sugar had on my skin picking urges, especially since I did not eat what I considered to be a lot of sugar. Within a week or so of giving it up, I felt almost no urges to pick.

Reducing or eliminating refined sugar is the number one dietary recommendation I make to my skin picking clients, and most find it as effective as I have. At first, and perhaps you are feeling the same way now, the thought of doing without sweet treats can be upsetting, like taking a favorite security blanket or teddy bear away from a small child. But I will reassure you as I reassure them - I'm not asking you to give it up forever. I suggest you do a trial elimination of sugar, for at least one or two weeks so you can notice what it feels like, and how your picking responds. Then you can make informed choices about eating sugar in the future, knowing fully the consequences. The results are typically dramatic, even if you don't cut out 100% of the sugar (such as in spaghetti sauce or other items, although I recommend you do). You will probably see, like my clients have, that your mood goes way up and your picking goes way down. You can expect to feel positive and energetic. A long-term depression may lift. You may stop picking entirely, like one of my clients who didn't pick until a box of cookies came in the mail. The next day, her depression returned, along with negative thoughts.

There is preliminary scientific support for the notion that ingesting sugar leads to skin picking. In a research study,[33] mice with a built-in tendency for skin picking types of behavior exhibited more of the behavior when fed a solution of tryptophan and sugar. The scientists were surprised - they expected the behavior to decrease because tryptophan is a precursor to serotonin, and this strain of mice have lower than normal levels of serotonin. The scientists had wanted to test the effects of increasing serotonin in the mice by adding tryptophan, and didn't think the sugar (added presumably to make it tasty enough for the mice to drink) would have an effect. Although the diet did raise serotonin levels, the mice "picked" more and some of the mice that had not been "picking" on a normal diet started picking on the high sugar/ high tryptophan diet.

Of course, since the scientists increased levels of tryptophan along with sugar, they cannot say conclusively that it was the sugar that increased the negative behavior, but the suggestion is so strong that I hope someone does the proper control experiment (testing the effect of sugar water as compared to regular water) and that we will see the results soon. Better yet would be a trial on human subjects. Yet, the only individuals equipped to do such research are doctors and psychologists in universities, and doctors are for the most part interested in testing drugs, while psychologists are interested in testing psychological therapies. So who is interested in testing the effects of sugar? I have to guess, unfortunately, no one. But luckily, you don't have to wait for the scientific research. Test it on yourself with an elimination diet.

Here are the basics of doing a sugar-elimination diet: Eat no sugar for at least a week, preferably two weeks. Keep the mini-log each evening - jot down a 0-10 rating for your overall mood that day, a 0-10 rating for your energy level, and a 0-10 rating for your picking. If you have other health problems, I recommend you include a rating for each of these as well, for example, joint pain or headaches. After the two weeks are over, allow yourself to eat sweets the next day. Continue keeping your mini-log and see what happens over the next couple of days.

Expect a challenge for the first couple of days of the elimination. You may feel intense cravings for sugar. In most cases, cravings for sugar come from eating sugar. In other words, sugar is the fuel for the sugar cravings. Depending on how much sugar they are used to eating, my clients typically report that the first two or three days of the elimination are somewhat difficult, and they feel crappy - low energy and even achy. After two or three days, the cravings ease or disappear and doing without sugar is relatively easy. By day six or seven, they notice they are feeling great, better than they can remember feeling in a long time. And because they are enjoying the happiness and energy, AND the freedom from picking urges, they come to the next sessions enthusiastic about a low-sugar diet, and curious to explore further dietary changes.

In some cases, sugar cravings are caused by nutritional deficiencies that need to be addressed, which we will discuss in the next section, "Are you getting enough?" Sometimes sugar cravings are merely a result of not eating enough food, period. If you are not getting enough, your body craves the most quickly digesting form of food: sugar. You may especially need to eat more fat and protein. Cravings can also be emotional. You may crave a piece of cake when you simply need a hug. Cravings may also kick in when we feel deprived. As you eliminate your picking behavior, part of you may feel deprived of the behavior that has caused you much anguish, but on the other hand has comforted you and eased your anxiety.

It is important not to give in too much to sugar cravings. While certain food cravings are caused by nutritional deficiency and should be indulged, cravings for sugar do not fall into this category. Remember that eating sugar is usually what is causing your cravings for sugar. Cravings for sugar should be resisted, or they will come back at least as strong the next day.

However, sugar is extremely addictive, (some research indicates about four times more addictive than cocaine!).[34] So if you are feeling like, "How can I ever hope to pull myself away from it, then?" be glad there are foods and supplements that make it much easier. Getting plenty of protein, good quality fat, and vegetables helps – especially sweet ones (like carrots), but you may also need amino acid supplements. In particular, 5-HTP, the direct biochemical precursor to serotonin (a neurotransmitter that is deficient in sufferers of depression and anxiety), helps reduce sugar cravings.[35]

Fermented foods like yogurt (unsweetened), kefir, sauerkraut, kimchee, kombucha can also help with sugar cravings. Or you can take probiotic pills, which will help too.

Just a note, if your sweet cravings are exclusively for chocolate, you might be in a state of magnesium deficiency. Magnesium is a crucial nutrient involved in hundreds of biochemical processes in the body, and is especially important for reducing anxiety,[36] which we know can be a huge contributor to picking. Since we need it more under stress, stress can deplete us of it, but so can sugar and caffeinated drinks (which to decrease our picking, we should avoid anyway). Seaweed, greens, avocado and nuts are good sources of magnesium, but you can also buy magnesium supplements.

Remember that it's not just candy, cakes, cookies, pastries and ice cream that have a boat-load of sugar. Drinks have an enormous amount, especially sweet coffee drinks, soda and energy drinks (even those with claims of being healthy). Read the ingredients and beware of other words for sugar as well. Stay away from corn syrup, dextrose, sucrose, fructose, and maltodextrin. Eliminate fruit juices as well. Without the fiber present in the whole fruit, the fruit sugars are absorbed way too quickly and behave similarly to refined sugar in soda. Diet soda is *not* a good replacement for regular soda. Its consumption can increase depression in sensitive individuals[37] and may contribute to many other health problems. In fact, 75% of the food complaints the FDA receives are about aspartame, the most common artificial sweetener.[38] What to drink? Water is your best option. Flavor it with lemon or lime juice if you like.

If you're already feeling deprived just imagining doing without your brownies or frappucinos, remember that there are still plenty of naturally sweet foods you can eat, even when you are eliminating refined sugar. Almost all fruits are sweet, as are plenty of vegetables, like sweet peas, carrots, beets, corn, sweet potatoes, pumpkins and acorn or kabocha squashes.

Okay, let's say you've already done the sugar elimination test and are motivated, having experienced the results, to keep your sugar intake low. You may be wondering whether you can have anything sweet, besides fruits and vegetables. The good news is that there are natural sweeteners that are less extreme than refined sugar, and you may be able to get away with eating them in small quantities. Raw honey, brown rice syrup and pure maple syrup are better alternatives to sugar. Stay away from honey that is not raw, though, as it has a high glycemic index similar to sugar. Uncooked (raw) honey has very opposite effects of sugar; it is anti-inflammatory as opposed to inflammatory and it appears to protect against cardiovascular disease, cancer and diabetes.[39] Agave is not a good choice.

A very sweet natural non-caloric alternative is stevia. It may taste odd to you at first, and I confess I don't like it at all in hot tea. However, I like it occasionally in lemonade, which requires a lot of sweetener to counter the lemon juice and would otherwise be off-limits.

Stimulants

Caffeine can make you antsy or anxious and thus have the effect of increasing your tendency to pick. If you drink coffee, soda, or even tea, experiment with reducing your caffeine intake. Cut back to green tea or water instead, and notice if you observe a positive effect. Caffeine also depletes you of vitamins like inositol,[40] which is a supplement that can be used to decrease picking (see supplements chapter), so you definitely want to make sure you have enough of it in your system.

Alcohol at first has a depressant, then a stimulant effect on the body. (That's why it can put you to sleep and then wake you up a few hours later.) Alcohol can have similar effects as sugar. If you drink, look out for a possible relationship between alcohol and increased picking. If you drink regularly, do an alcohol elimination, just as described for the sugar, and observe the results.

Other foods can trigger picking. Yogis avoid rajasic foods, foods which are said to be activating to the mind, because they make sitting peacefully and stilling the mind in meditation much more difficult. These foods may agitate you and increase your picking – experiment and notice. In addition to coffee and refined sugar, rajasic foods include garlic, onions, chili peppers and hot sauce. Personally, I noticed garlic and onions seemed to have the effect of making me pick more, but we are all different, so I encourage you to notice which foods may lead to increased picking for you.

There is a diet specifically developed to reduce hair pulling, and it is used for skin picking too. Developed by John Kender, called the John Kender diet, it is based on the hypothesis that picking and pulling occurs when oils on the skin are broken down by a species of yeast living on the skin into compounds that irritate our skin or hair. Foods like sugar and others cause an overgrowth of yeast, while other foods, according to Kender, keep the yeast in check. The hypothesis has not been tested scientifically, but you can find a list of "good" foods and "bad" foods online. I think it is likely that there are several different causes of skin picking, and one might be an overgrowth of this yeast. If you are up for experimenting more with your food, it might be worthwhile to try this diet.

Wheat and milk

Sensitivity or intolerance to wheat or dairy products is extremely common these days. You may have a problem with either or both, while being completely unaware of it. It may even be contributing to your picking. A few of my clients have discovered wheat was affecting their picking as well as contributing to other health problems.

Why is it happening that so many of us cannot handle wheat and dairy anymore? First wheat. Nowadays wheat in America is completely different than it was just two generations ago. It has been hybridized to contain much more wheat gluten, a protein that helps make bread fluffy and chewy. Our digestive systems are not the same as they used to be and, in fact, they are often severely compromised. A healthy gut is flush with trillions of beneficial bacterial cells, which are integral to the gut and actually help us digest our food with their enzymes. A major part of our immune system comes from the gut as well, and the gut flora (bacteria) actually protect us from getting sick. These days, for many reasons, including antibiotics, birth control pills, sugar and stress, our gut flora is likely to be less than optimal. Opportunistic and even pathogenic organisms have replaced the beneficial bacteria.

This suboptimal flora may not even line the intestines properly. The result is a "leaky gut," in which incompletely digested protein fragments are able to pass through the wall of the small intestine and are absorbed into the blood stream. These fragments, called peptides, then cause trouble. The immune system sees them and knows they are not supposed to be there, so it attacks them. This is an inflammatory response, and we know that inflammation is a cause of not only aches and pains, but the major degenerative diseases that we are typically dying from. The peptides also resemble certain types of cells in the body, and over time the immune system is primed to even attack those parts of the body, resulting in autoimmune diseases, also extremely common these days.

The peptides are also toxic to the brain. In Natasha Campbell-McBride's book "Gut and Psychology Syndrome" (GAPS), she makes a convincing case for this being the mechanism for autism, learning disabilities and mental disorders, including schizophrenia and OCD.[41] Since compulsive skin picking is so similar to OCD, GAPS may play a role in skin picking as well. Extrapolating from my experience coaching skin pickers to test these foods, I would guess that many who pick have a problem with wheat and some with dairy as well.

But "bread is so comforting and makes me feel good," you may be saying to yourself. That is because, to counter the inflammatory response, the adrenal glands pump out endorphins, which give us a "high." They make us feel good. You may even be addicted to wheat, because of the endorphin release.

The more you love bread, and the more you eat wheat-based cereals and pastas, bagels and all sorts of bread and baked goods, the more likely it is that you have developed an intolerance to gluten. Are you tired or achy a lot? Get headaches, even migraines? Feel "brain fog?" Joints hurt? Overweight but can't lose the pounds? Do you have bumps on the backs of your arms (keratosis pilaris)? These all can be symptoms of gluten intolerance, although there are many other symptoms.[42] Worse, do you have an autoimmune disease like Hashimoto's thyroiditis, alopecia, excema, lupus, rheumatoid arthritis? Gluten sensitivity is a causative factor in some autoimmune diseases (in which your immune system attacks your own body), because the immune system gets so revved up attacking the gluten protein that it starts attacking proteins in your body that resemble it. Even if you have no other physical or mental problems other than the skin picking (rare, and if this is the case I'm guessing you're young), I strongly recommend a wheat elimination test diet. Following the same protocol as for sugar (above), notice how you feel without it and then add it back in to test how you react to it after your body is cleansed of it for at least two weeks.

Dairy, and in particular the dairy protein casein, is the second most common food component to cause problems. I recommend you try a dairy elimination diet as well. In fact, you can combine the two; have no wheat or dairy for two weeks, then on day 15 add wheat back in. If you feel fine, add dairy back in on day 18. If you feel badly from the wheat on days 15-17, remove it again, then add dairy back when you feel better. You may even wish to test other common allergenic foods at the same time, such as citrus, soy and eggs. Just be sure you only add back in one food at a time, so you can be sure of the results.

If you do discover that you are not tolerating certain foods, eliminate them completely. Although beyond the scope of this book, you may be able to heal your gut so that in the future you can tolerate the foods. Eliminating processed foods, eating plenty of fresh vegetables, and eliminating sugar and probably wheat and/or dairy is still important, but you may need to go further to heal your gut.[43]

Dairy is highly praised in Ayurveda. However, Ayurveda was developed in ancient India, and dairy has become a totally different thing in modern America, where most milk products are from "factory farms," in which cows are fed an unnatural diet of corn or other grains instead of grass, and are pumped full of hormones and antibiotics. Even if you are not lactose intolerant or allergic to milk protein (casein), if you tend to have acne, PMS, painful periods or other female reproductive problems, it is best to eliminate milk products. If you are unsure of this, do at least a one-month elimination and notice how you feel.

In case you have already been tested for food allergies, note that common allergy tests look only for acute allergic reaction, while the delayed response we are talking about here involves a different type of antibody (IgG or IgA rather than IgE). So just because it doesn't show up on a test does not mean you don't have a problem. The elimination diet is the best way to find out.

Processed Foods

For your overall health, not specifically related to skin picking, but not necessarily unrelated either, eliminate as much processed foods as you can. The best food to buy does not have "ingredients," rather it is only one thing. An apple is an apple, no ingredients needed. Any apple sauce or apple pie you make from the apple is going to be healthier than the corresponding item you would buy in the grocery store (or worse, at a convenience store or fast food place). It is always better to eat unprocessed foods, to eat from the edges of the grocery store, rather than from the packaged goods in the middle. However, if you are eating some processed convenience foods, look at the ingredients. Some are better choices than others. Especially stay away from artificial colors and flavors – don't eat ingredients named with a color and a number. There is evidence that such dyes are harmful and contribute to ADHD and other mental and physical conditions.[44] I would not be surprised if they contribute to skin picking as well. Unfortunately, while these ingredients are banned in many countries, in the United States we cannot trust our government to protect us, because agencies such as the Food and Drug Administration (FDA) and the U.S. Department of Agriculture (USDA) are heavily influenced by the food and drug companies, who financially support and lobby legislators and act only in their business interests. We need to be informed and look out for our own health.

The oils and fats in processed foods are unhealthful. They are either hydrogenated fats (contain the terrible-for-you trans fats), or vegetable oils like sunflower and safflower oil. These oils, even when they are not rancid (making them very unhealthy), are omega-6 fats. We eat far too much omega-6 fats, and they are not what we need for healthy brain structure.

Finally, in yogic terms, packaged processed food is considered extremely tamasic, low energy, dulling food. Filled with various chemical ingredients, it lacks the life-force that fresh foods do, and it robs us of our energy.

In summary, to balance your body and reduce your physical tendency towards picking, remove from your diet: sugar, artificial sweeteners, as much processed foods as possible, and any food you are sensitive to, as determined by an elimination diet. You may wish to minimize alcohol, caffeine and other rajasic food as well.

Food: Are you getting enough of these?

Stable blood sugar is an important factor in keeping down your body's tendency to "need" to pick. (That may be why sugar causes increased picking, because of its tendency to destabilize blood sugar.)

Regarding stable blood sugar, first consider whether you are getting enough food in general, and at regular meals. For some of my clients, simply adding breakfast if they were not in the habit of eating it, or a real lunch instead of a carbohydrate snack, made a *huge* difference in reducing their picking, even when their picking happened late in the day or even at night.

If you need to go many hours between meals - perhaps if you work late or have a long commute - be sure you have some healthy snacks with you. Getting too hungry can be a trigger for picking.

That said, regular meals are the best way to go. Contrary to popular belief in recent years that it is healthy to eat many small meals, it actually *is* preferable to eat three regular meals rather than frequent smaller meals (grazing) all day. Getting enough protein and fat at these meals will stabilize your blood sugar, so you won't be hungry for a few hours. Remember our introduction to

Ayurveda in the sense therapies chapter, where we spoke about controlling the vata energy to reduce picking? Vata is controlled by regularity, of meals as well as other elements of our lifestyle, so it makes sense to eat fewer, regular substantial meals. It is even a better plan if you would like to lose weight. A recent study showed that people lost more weight on two large meals a day than on six small ones.[45]

We also need to eat appropriately for the climate and season. Remember that vata is the quality of quick, cold and dry that causes anxiety and nervous behaviors. So according to Ayurveda and common sense, if you live in a four seasons climate, an appropriate diet for winter is warm cooked foods and a lot of nourishing soups and stews. I have known health-minded people eating cold smoothies and salads in the frigid Midwest winter. They thought they were being healthy, but instead they were aggravating vata, and as a result were plagued by anxiety and insomnia. Only in the summer would I recommend skin pickers eat raw or cold foods. Also, to reduce excess vata, you should avoid dry crunchy foods, even though your vata nature might draw you to them! A diet needs to be balanced, which means not only eating a variety of foods, but also paying attention to their energetic qualities. Meats and cheeses are densely nutritive and have an extremely contractive energy, a heavy quality, while fish is a little less contractive. Sugars and caffeine are extremely expansive – they make us feel light and happy and energized, temporarily at least. It is easier to stay in balance if the majority of our food is moderately, rather than extremely, expansive or contractive. For example, green leafy vegetables that grow up towards the sun are moderately expansive; they lift our energy and make us feel light, but not in an extreme way. Root vegetables that grow down into the earth are moderately contractive. They are grounding (and good to balance vata) even though many can also provide the sweet taste we crave in a more moderate form than refined sweets.

After a few weeks of a balanced diet that is low in sugar and densely caloric processed foods, your tastes will change. Healthy fruits and vegetables then taste amazingly sweet and delicious, while most cakes and candies begin to taste too sweet, and overly-salted processed food too salty.

Protein

Neurotransmitters, chemical messengers in the brain and nervous system, are derived from aromatic amino acids, found in abundant amounts only in animal based foods. They are crucial for keeping us calm, focused, and happy, but how many of us are not? *So many*, judging from the sales of SSRI antidepressants, which aim to keep levels of the neurotransmitter serotonin up to a desirable level. But why are so many of us anxious and depressed? One reason can be once again, our suboptimal gut flora. A large amount of our neurotransmitters, including 95% of our serotonin, are made by the beneficial bacteria in our gut, so we may not have enough of the right kind of bacteria to efficiently make them.

Also, some of us may not be eating enough protein to make sufficient levels of neurotransmitters from the key amino acids. Problems with depression, anxiety and picking could be in part a result of amino acid deficiency. Julia Ross, in "The Mood Cure," recommends at least 20 grams of protein at each meal for proper neurotransmitter support. (Vegetarians need to be careful eaters in order to get this amount of protein.) Ross is also a proponent of amino acid therapy, which we'll discuss in the supplements chapter.

Vegetables and fruits

Vegetables and fruits are key, and most of us don't get nearly enough. Eating more vegetables not only prevents chronic physical diseases, but a recent large scale study found that people's happiness and mental health was greater the more servings of vegetables and fruits they ate per day, topping off at seven servings.[46] In other words, no further benefit was found from eight or nine. Fruits and vegetables are classified as sattvic in Ayurveda, meaning they have a high, pure energy that we can all use more of. Julia Ross recommends 8-12 cups of vegetables daily. Salad greens only count half as much, because most of the volume is air!

Take a good look at your diet. If you eat bread or cereal for breakfast, a sandwich and chips for lunch, and pasta for dinner, you are getting 1) way too many grain-based carbohydrates, 2) not enough protein and 3) not enough vegetables. It is a mood and picking disaster.

Fat

Fat is an incredibly important nutrient that has gotten an undeserved and lingering bad reputation, although it has been exonerated by medical science. Even saturated fat and cholesterol are not the villains they were once thought to be.

Every cell in your body has a membrane around it that is made up of mostly fat, and your brain is around sixty percent fat. Omega-3 fats are the most important fats for the brain to have, yet they are not nearly as common in our diets as omega-6 fats are. We intake a much higher ratio of omega 6 to omega 3 fats than we should, due to the oils in processed foods, cooking with vegetable oils (although olive oil, an omega-9 source, is healthy), and to factory farmed meats, which mainly have omega-6 as a result of the animals eating an unnatural grain-based diet, rather than the grass they have always grazed on in the past.

Omega 3 fats are anti-inflammatory and are thus important for preventing all the common modern disease killers that used to be rare. They also help reduce acne, due to their anti-inflammatory nature.

What effect do they have on our fat brain? A high ratio of omega-6 to omega-3 is correlated with depression. Adding omega-3 fats to the diet has been shown to have a positive impact on depression, bipolar disorder, ADHD, schizophrenia and maybe Alzheimer's.[47] Omega-3 increases brain levels of antidepressant neurotransmitters dopamine and serotonin by inhibiting the MAO enzymes that destroy them.

The best source of omega-3 naturally is fatty cold-water fish, particularly wild-caught salmon, sardines, anchovies, herring and mackerel. There are also high omega-3 eggs now. Grass-fed beef is also a source, but can be expensive. If you are a vegetarian, flaxseeds have a substantial amount of one type of omega-3, and other seeds and nuts have some amount, walnuts being the best of those. However, while the flaxseed omegas are good for the heart, only about one-third of us can use flax seed oil to benefit our brains; the rest of us do not have enough of the enzymes needed to convert it to the usable form.[48] Algae oil is a better option for vegetarians, as algae do contain the kind of omega-3 the brain can use. Fish get *their* omega-3s from algae.

Water

We are never at our best when we are dehydrated. Water is like "brain juice," and without it we can feel sluggish and experience "brain fog." It can pep you up but also calm you down. Our requirements for water vary depending on our size, the nature of our diet and what we drink, how much we sweat, and on how much stress we are under. We need more water under stressful conditions. If we eat a poor diet consisting of processed packaged foods, or fast foods that are light on vegetables, those foods are relatively dry and we will need even more water. Caffeinated and alcoholic drinks also act as diuretics, causing us to eliminate water. If you drink these, you would need even more water. Assuming a good diet, the common recommendation of eight 8-ounce glasses of water per day is probably a good one.[49] Even if you are drinking teas or juices, the body still benefits from additional pure water.

Summary

Facing the prospect of changing your diet can be overwhelming. If your stress level went skyrocketing simply reading the last two chapters, please take a deep breath and know you don't have to make changes all at once, and in fact that is not what I would recommend. Take small manageable steps. As you incorporate positive food changes, they will become easier and habitual and you will find you have more energy for added changes. A health coach is very helpful in this regard, helping you implement changes in ways that will work, custom-tailored for you.

Dietary supplements

For many reasons it is rare today for *anyone* to be ingesting the optimal levels of all nutrients. Most of us readily admit we do not eat as well as we should. Even when we do, most of the soil that our produce and grains are grown on is depleted in a variety of nutrients compared to the soil of the past. Even livestock are generally not freely grazing on quality natural grasses, but are fed grains, like corn, which are grown on depleted soil and are too high in omega-6 fatty acids and too low in healthy omega-3s. Additionally, modern life is highly stressful. Under stress we use up certain vitamins at a higher rate, so we need to ingest more of them.

A sizable component of your skin picking may be physically based and will likely respond to altering your diet and adding supplements. Some supplements will need to be taken only temporarily until any imbalance or deficiency is corrected, while others should be used routinely.

Supplements everyone ought to be taking:

A Multivitamin

Almost nobody gets enough of all the vitamins and minerals needed for optimal health. And many vitamins and minerals are of special concern to those who pick their skin: some are important to healing scars, others for fighting acne, and still others for our mental well-being. I highly recommend taking a multivitamin every day.

Supplements most of us will need:

Vitamin D

Sometimes called the "sunshine vitamin" because it is made in our skin upon exposure to sunlight, most of us suffer from insufficient amounts of vitamin D, which is a serious concern. "Current research indicates vitamin D deficiency plays a role in causing seventeen varieties of cancer as well as heart disease, stroke, hypertension, autoimmune diseases, diabetes, depression, chronic pain, osteoarthritis, osteoporosis, muscle weakness, muscle wasting, birth defects and periodontal disease," says John Jacob Cannell, MD, the founder of the non-profit Vitamin D Council.

Skin disorders like psoriasis and eczema are often treated with vitamin D creams or UV light therapy. Some skin pickers have keratosis pilaris, tiny bumps most commonly on the backs of the upper arms, which also may improve with vitamin D.

How do you know whether you are deficient in vitamin D? One low-tech test: press your fingertips firmly into your sternum (breastbone). If it hurts, you are probably extremely low in vitamin D. There is also a blood test for vitamin D3; ask your doctor for it.

It is nearly impossible to get sufficient vitamin D from our food. Milk is supplemented with vitamin D2, less beneficial than vitamin D3, and in the amount that only prevents rickets, the acute vitamin D deficiency disease, but not enough for the cancer protection and other benefits. Moderate sun exposure in the summer, 10 to 15 minutes midday (without sunscreen) is a good amount – not enough to turn you pink. However, most of us live at too high a latitude to get any significant amount of sun in the winter, so supplementing is most likely necessary for a few months at least (*especially* if you tend to experience seasonal depression). Cod liver oil is one good way of supplementing vitamin D. Or take specific vitamin D3 supplements. Liquid or capsule form is best. Take with food containing fat for best absorption. Since it is a fat-soluble vitamin, you **can** get too much of it. When in doubt, follow the instructions on the bottle and get your blood tested periodically.

Omega-3 fats

The benefits of omega-3 fats were discussed in the previous chapter. Unless you are eating fish at least five times a week, consider supplementing with fish oil or krill oil, which may be even better.[50] If you are strictly vegetarian, use flaxseed oil or, preferably, algae oil. Experts disagree on how much to take, but probably at least 1000 mg (1g) is appropriate (some recommend 4000mg or more). Because these oils thin the blood, if you are taking more, be sure you are getting plenty of vitamin K (abundant in leafy greens) to support blood clotting.

Probiotics

If you have taken a lot of antibiotics in your lifetime, or even birth control pills (or even if your mother did), chances are you have sub-optimal gut flora. What? As discussed earlier, proper digestion of our food in the small intestine depends on beneficial bacteria. These bacteria help break down proteins into amino acids, which are then absorbed into the bloodstream and distributed to fulfill our bodies' needs. Antibiotic medicines are typically indiscriminate in their destruction of bacteria, and when the beneficial bacteria are gone, the gut may be repopulated with neutral or harmful bacteria or fungal organisms. These other organisms do not have the enzymes to break down proteins we ingest, so what happens is they are only partially broken down into peptides, which are absorbed into the blood because of "leaky gut." Some of the peptides are psychoactive and addictive.[51] For example, peptides derived from incompletely digested wheat gluten and milk casein proteins act like morphine. These peptides are also targets of the immune system, and allergies develop as a result. People are often addicted to the very foods to which they are allergic. Since pathogenic gut flora contribute to autism, schizophrenia, ADD, OCD, autoimmune diseases,[52] and I believe it can contribute to skin picking as well.

What to do? For one thing, you can reintroduce beneficial bacteria in the form of aggressive probiotics. Store bought yogurt and other fermented foods typically do not have strains that are sufficiently aggressive to supplant the bacteria and fungi (such as yeast) that are already in your intestines. If you are not ambitious enough to make homemade yogurt or sauerkraut, you can buy probiotic supplements. Look for one containing several species of lactobacilli, bifidobacteria, and if possible, bacillis subtilis. You may recognize them listed as L. something or B. something where the "somethings" can be a number of different species – for example L. acidophilus is a common lactobacteria; B. bifidum a common bifidobacteria. Buy a supplement that provides at least 15 billion bacterial cells per capsule.

Start taking the probiotic very gradually. Open a capsule and take a small amount of it with or after food. If a probiotic is strong enough to be working properly, what happens is it will cause a die-off of the undesirable organisms in your gut. Those organisms release toxins as they die off and you may actually see a temporary worsening of your symptoms for a few days or even possibly longer. Or you may simply feel very tired. If you see no symptoms, or when the symptoms disappear, then you can increase the dose and take more probiotic the next day. Slowly work your way up until you are ingesting 15-50 billion cells per day. Depending on the severity of your skin picking or digestive issues, you may need to take this dose daily for several months, perhaps even a year or two. It takes a while to build a new stable population of bacteria in your gut. If your problems return, you can always go back to taking the probiotics.

More specialized supplements you may find helpful:

Consult with your doctor or pharmacist before trying any of the following over-the-counter supplements, especially *if you are already taking medication for depression or anxiety.*

N-acetylcysteine (NAC)

Of substances that have been tested scientifically, N-acetylcysteine (NAC) has proven the most effective in reducing compulsive hair pulling. Many individuals have reported that it works for their skin picking as well. Medications such as SSRI antidepressants have not proven as effective. NAC is an amino acid that modulates the amount of the neurotransmitter glutamate in the brain. In a 12-week placebo controlled double-blind study,[53] 56% of the participants experienced a significant reduction in hair pulling compared to only 16% of participants who were given the placebo.

NAC helped only slightly more than half the people in the small study, so there is no guarantee that it is going to help you. However, it is considered safe and is relatively inexpensive, so you may decide you would like to try it.

Although widely available in health food stores and online, it is a good idea to consult with your doctor and/or pharmacist before trying supplements, particularly if you take medication.

To try NAC, you would start with one 600 mg capsule in the morning and one at night, or if your skin picking is only a problem in the evening, you can take both capsules then. After two weeks, you can go up to four capsules per day (2400 mg). This is the level that was tested in the study. If you feel fine, after two more weeks, you may choose to go up to six capsules a day (3600 mg daily). Stay at 2400 or 3600 mg per day. It will take a few weeks to notice results. In the hair pulling study, it took nine weeks to see significant improvement, although a couple of my clients reported positive results in less than half that time. Always supplement with a vitamin C pill and a multivitamin. The body needs much more vitamin C and possibly also more minerals when taking NAC. Possible side effects include nausea and digestive upset.

Inositol

There have been small studies on OCD, depression, anxiety, and compulsive hair pulling and skin picking showing the B-complex vitamin inositol to be helpful. Fred Penzel, Ph.D. has also seen it work in several hair pulling and skin picking patients in his clinic and writes about how you would try it for skin picking[54].

If you would like to take inositol, consult with your physician. Do not take it if you are taking lithium. Inositol is best taken in powdered form, dissolved into water or juice. Mix well and let it sit 10 minutes to more fully dissolve. Start with 4 grams per day, divided into 2 doses (1 teaspoon each dose). If you are tolerating it well, work your way up over a number of weeks, including a third dose, to a maximum of 18 grams per day. Possible side effects include gas and diarrhea. When you reach 18 grams or the maximum you can comfortably tolerate, stay at that dosage for six weeks to evaluate whether it works to decrease your unwanted behaviors. If it does not help over a period of six weeks, it is unlikely to be of use to you. I would suggest tapering it down, rather than stopping cold-turkey.

5-HTP

5-hydroxytryptophan (5-HTP), a natural precursor to serotonin, has been available as a supplement in the United States since 1997. Too little serotonin in the brain is a well-known and widespread problem. SSRI drugs such as Prozac have been the pharmaceutical answer to this problem but they do not work as cleanly, without side effects, as simply taking the natural biochemical precursor 5-HTP and allowing the body to make serotonin from it.

5-HTP supplementation has demonstrated effectiveness on depression, sleep problems, binge eating and weight loss and can alleviate certain painful conditions (depending on the cause) such as fibromyalgia, TMJ pain and migraines.[55] They likely reduce anxiety,[56] and obsessive-compulsive type behaviors. I believe they are likely to help skin picking too, although that has not been scientifically tested.

5-HTP works quickly, sometimes within 10 minutes. Julia Ross in her book The Mood Cure recommends taking it mid-afternoon and just before bed. As she suggests, start with 50 mg and if you don't feel better in an hour, take another 50 mg capsule. If you still feel no response after another hour, take a final 50 mg capsule. Whatever your total dose, repeat it in the evening just before bed (so you are taking no more than 300 mg in a day.) If you don't notice positive changes within a week, or if you experience negative side effects (some people feel queasy or sleep restlessly), stop taking it and consider trying tryptophan or Saint-John's Wort. If 5-HTP *is* effective, take a short break every time you finish a bottle to test whether you still need it. (If you feel worse, continue with another bottle.) Headaches can be a sign that you don't need it anymore (so stop *before* you finish the bottle). As long as you are eating well, getting enough protein and important vitamins in your diet, you are not in a deficient state anymore and therefore shouldn't need it again.

Tryptophan

Tryptophan is an amino acid that is present in the protein that you ingest. It is converted to 5-HTP, which is converted to serotonin. So, if 5-HTP doesn't work for you, it may be worthwhile to try tryptophan supplements. Tryptophan has an interesting story of usage. It was commonly prescribed for depression by psychiatrists and other doctors in the '80s because it was very effective. For this reason, when Prozac initially came on the market in 1989, Eli Lilly had a difficult time selling it, until a Japanese amino acid manufacturer sent a contaminated batch of tryptophan to the United States that killed over forty people. Although there were other makers of tryptophan, people were afraid to buy it, and sales of Prozac, and similar drugs that followed, soared. Although tryptophan was used continually in other countries, and never made again by the manufacturer of the contaminated batch, it was not available again in the US until 1995 (with a doctor's prescription). In 2000 tryptophan became available in the US *without* a prescription.

Besides depression, tryptophan can be used for all the conditions mentioned above in the 5-HTP section. Additionally it has been shown to help PMS,[57] and veterinarians use it to treat obsessive-compulsive parrots who pluck out their own feathers.

If you want to try tryptophan, the recommended dose is 500mg in the midafternoon and 500mg at bedtime. (Similar to 5-HTP, if you don't notice effects from one 500 mg pill, you can do a second, wait and see if you need a third.)

Saint-John's Wort

This is an herb, comparable or better in effectiveness to Prozac.[58] If 5-HTP or tryptophan don't work for you,

Saint-John's-Wort might. If you would like to try it, Julia Ross recommends 300 mg at lunch and 300 mg with dinner. If you have sleeping troubles, you can take a third dose before bed.

Other supplements for neurotransmitter support:

You may be deficient in other neurotransmitters, and there are a few other amino acid supplements that you may find helpful. For example, GABA can help calm you down. (GABA also increases naturally by practicing yoga or meditation.) To learn more about them I highly recommend the book "The Mood Cure" by Julia Ross, M.A.

Section 6 - Other Concerns

Acne

Not everyone picks because of acne, but many skin pickers are plagued with acne and find that they feel less need to pick when there is objectively less to pick at. Almost everyone will pick at or pop the occasional pimple. Though not all skin pickers pick at acne, many find it to be an intense trigger and do pick less when their skin is clearer.

Acne is highly diet dependent, a fact which many people, including doctors, are not aware. There are many scientific studies correlating dietary changes with acne improvements. What are the top dietary considerations to address?

Inflammation

Acne is a product of inflammation. Most of our chronic diseases are caused by inflammation, and acne is no exception. Avoid foods that promote inflammation, particularly hydrogenated or trans fats, saturated fats, and also vegetable oils that are high in omega-6 fatty acids like corn, sunflower, safflower, and soybean oil. Many of these substances are found in processed foods and snacks. It is always a good idea to minimize these.

195

On the other hand, omega-3 fatty acids lower inflammation, especially eicosapentanoic acid (EPA) from fish, so eating more cold-water fish like wild-caught salmon, sardines, mackerel and herring and/or taking fish oil supplements can help reduce acne.[59] Vegetarian sources like flax oil, walnuts and cold-pressed canola oil can work too, but must be converted to EPA via enzymes that require vitamin B6, vitamin C, magnesium, zinc and niacin, so you must be sure you are getting enough of these vitamins and minerals.

Antioxidants also help prevent inflammation, so that includes NAC, vitamins A, C, E, minerals such as selenium and zinc, and also many other antioxidant substances found only in fruits (especially berries) and vegetables, and in red and black beans. Green tea is another good source of antioxidants. There are also antioxidants in black tea, coffee and dark chocolate, although these have undesirable stimulant effects. Many spices have antioxidants, but usually are not eaten in sufficient amounts to have an effect. Turmeric is one of the best anti-inflammatory spices and can be taken in larger amounts. Try taking one or two teaspoons of turmeric, mix it into hot water and drink in the morning as a tea. It's not the best-tasting tea, but not the worst tasting "medicine" either. Fresh ginger is also good, and makes a tasty, spicy tea. Cut up a few slices and boil for a few minutes.

Dairy

Epidemiological studies show a clear correlation between dairy intake and acne.[60] Recent research is also showing causation, that removing milk or milk proteins from peoples' diet causes the acne to decrease or disappear.[61] Some dermatologists include dairy reduction in their prescriptions and have seen thousands of patients benefit. Milk is designed to help baby animals grow rapidly, and so has growth hormones, which stimulate the production of sebum, the substance that clogs the pores and causes acne. Milk also triggers insulin release and elevates the levels of insulin-like growth factor (IGF-1) in the blood, which has also been implicated in acne.[62] Cows treated with bovine growth hormone (rBGH) may produce milk with even higher levels of IGF-1, so if you *are* drinking milk, buy organic milk from cows raised without rBGH.

If you are a heavy consumer of dairy products, you can try reducing your intake. That may help, or it may be more effective to eliminate them completely from your diet. If you are not sure how dairy affects you, you can do a temporary elimination diet, removing dairy for a couple of weeks before reintroducing it and noticing the effects.

Glycemic Index

Foods with a high glycemic index (ability to quickly raise blood sugar) including sugar, juices, and certain carbohydrate foods that are quickly digested such as potatoes, trigger a rise in insulin and IGF-1, causing acne by a similar mechanism as dairy. Reducing your consumption of foods with a high glycemic index and eating more foods of low glycemic index can go a long way to clearing up your skin.

Stress

Stress is a contributing factor towards acne.[63] Stress increases inflammation, so along with an anti-inflammatory diet, make efforts to reduce stress, and you will reduce your acne. Exercise, get enough sleep, practice yoga and/or meditation, spend time in nature, and have fun. Laugh a lot.

Topical Acne Treatments

Studies show the effectiveness of tea tree oil, a natural antibiotic for acne.[64] A 5% tea tree oil gel was found to be as effective (albeit slower-acting) and have less side effects than benzoyl peroxide, the most common topical acne medication.[65] 5% is 1 part pure tea tree oil to 19 parts water. You probably need to shake it up well, and don't worry if your measurements are not exact.

Acne medications

As a holistic health practitioner, I see acne as a symptom of a whole system out of balance, and would therefore always recommend holistic modifications to the diet and lifestyle before using acne medications, which have potentially dangerous side effects.

Hormones

Have you noticed a connection between your picking and your hormones? For many women, picking started or worsened in adolescence when we began having menstrual cycles. (For some, that may be because of the onset of acne.) Occasionally, some women *start* picking around the time of menopause, or mild picking worsens. You may have noticed the severity of your picking to be hormonally related, becoming worse in the week or so before your menstrual period. This is extremely common, and in the case of hair pulling, was confirmed in a scientific study.[66] If we have PMS, we might feel completely out of control and not like our usual selves. In my mid-thirties, I used to observe that everything bad that happened in my life happened in the week or two before my period.

But PMS is not inevitable. It is another sign of imbalance. When our bodies are truly in balance, PMS goes away. Proper diet can help, especially eliminating dairy and perhaps using medicinal herbs. Another simple yet profound tool to use is acupressure. If you have terrible PMS or menstrual cramps and you're willing to do just a bit of work each month, I highly recommend the book "Woman Heal Thyself[67]" by Jeanne Elizabeth Blum. For two decades I had irregular periods, and for a few years in my mid-thirties, I had terrible PMS. I would experience heightened negative emotions, particularly fear and anger, as well as painfully sore breasts. (I also had ovarian cysts, which disappeared after a month or two of regular acu*puncture* treatments.) Then, following Blum's book, I started doing a few minutes of acupressure massage three days a month, and for the last five or six years my periods have been regular. Also, my PMS and negative emotions, breast soreness and out-of-control compulsiveness and picking are gone. Overall, my reproductive cycle is more regular and balanced in my 40's than it was in my 20's and 30's. Another must-read for women is "Balance Your Hormones, Balance Your Life[68]" by Dr. Claudia Welch, MSOM.

Staying motivated

It is human nature to be enthusiastic when starting a new endeavor, and then with time… that enthusiasm wanes. Especially if the endeavor takes sustained effort and energy. Stopping picking requires continual effort. It's a bit like running up a really long escalator that is going down. If we let up the pressure and stop for a few moments, we may find ourselves feeling like we are right back at the beginning. After a time, it does get easier, but it isn't something that can be accomplished in a week or even a month. But no effort is ever lost. Even at those times when you feel like you're back to square one, you have not un-done everything. You have learned something.

It's also human nature for us to need each other. This is not a weakness, so please don't think of it as such, if you find that you don't seem to be able to stop picking on your own, or can't even seem to implement any of the suggestions in this book. You may need support, motivation and accountability from another person or a group. You may choose to hire a professional therapist, counselor or coach.

The best thing about coaching is having someone tell you what to work on. I typically give my clients 1-3 recommendations to focus on in the weeks between sessions. If you cannot afford coaching or therapy, you still have options to get help from people.

Another best thing about coaching or counseling is simply having someone to be accountable to. Think about it: without assignments or tests in school, how much would you have studied? Without a boss or the need for money, how much would you work? Less, right? We do much better at whatever it is we are doing if we have some form of motivation and accountability, so if you don't hire someone for this purpose, you may need to find another means of accountability in order to create more success at stopping picking.

There are hundreds of people on Facebook and twitter and skin picking support forums who are potential buddies. Put it out there and find a buddy, or even a group to work with, using this book as a guide. If you want, tweet your message (looking for an accountability buddy) to me @Annettep333 and I will retweet it to my followers.

There are also in-person support groups. See trich.org for a list of current groups. There may be one in your town. If not, you will also find advice and support on trich.org for starting one. They will even inform everyone on their mailing list from your area that there is a new group starting. It can be an even better motivator if you start one yourself, because it will get you to be there at every meeting! It will be your responsibility to be there and keep the group going, which can keep you on track. Plus, it's good karma to help others. The benefits you give by hosting a group will also benefit you.

As far as other ways to stay motivated, remember your "pros of not picking" list. You may want to hang that up somewhere, or keep it at your bedside and look at it each morning or evening. Whatever works best for you.

Reminders can help too. For example, you can put post-its in your prime picking spots, reminding you with helpful phrases like, "eyes away," "hands away" or "What do you really want?" You may want to put up pictures or make a vision board - of clear skin, or of something that represents the feeling of freedom you are trying to achieve. Then you will have a visual reminder of what you really want.

If you find you are back-sliding, ask yourself why. Have you stopped keeping even a mini-log? Get back on that horse. Eating sugar again? There you go. Used to do breathing exercises, but have been slacking off lately?

You may find you need to try new strategies every once in a while. Things change; reminder post-its become invisible, the tangle toy that worked so well at first doesn't hold your interest anymore. Try something new. Perhaps you've never done hypnosis tapes, or haven't tried going gluten-free, or you need a new way to keep your hands busy. Read this book again whenever you feel you need a boost in motivation or some new insight. Chances are you will find some information you didn't use before, or some key techniques that you forgot and need to be reminded about.

Another way to to inspire you to continue doing the work is to use the book "Pearls: Meditations on Hair Pulling and Skin Picking" by Christine Pearson. Each page is a stand-alone reading, so you can go through it bit by bit, perhaps a page a day, either upon waking or just before you go to bed.

We all hit plateaus of progress, and there will be times in your life you won't want to put so much energy into this. Times when you are busy with other things in your life that you prefer to focus on, things that will matter more to you at that time, especially if you have made a lot of progress and reduced your picking to the point where it is not the problem it used to be. It may not bother you at all, and that's great. You can live a wonderful full life without ever completely stopping your picking. There's no reason to obsess over doing it when it doesn't really impact your life.

But if you're not satisfied with your progress yet, remember that persistence is the key, and practice. Instead of the adage, "Practice makes perfect," I prefer the phrases that two of my teachers used. My old dance teacher would always say, "Practice makes better." How can you argue with that? My fitness instructor is fond of, "Practice makes permanent." It is true that, with enough effort of repetition, you can change your body, mind and behavior. That's what you've been doing for so long: practicing picking. Now to counter the "permanence," you have to do a lot of practicing other things to get you to stop picking.

Finally regarding persistence, one of my favorite quotes is by 20th century scientist William Lawrence Bragg: "If you go on hammering away at a problem, it seems to get tired, lies down and lets you catch it." So by all means, hammer away at this challenge from all directions. Tell it you will not let up until it falls down and lets you catch it.

Thank you for reading this book. I wish you all the best in your journey. Remember, it's not easy, but you can absolutely do it!

Resources

Stopskinpickingcoach.com This is my website. Go there now to receive a free report, newsletter and video instructing the breathing exercise I teach in the pranayama chapter.

Trich.org The website of the Trichotillomania Learning Center, a nonprofit organization offering comprehensive information about skin picking and other BFRBs, including a list of therapists trained to treat them. They also have great educational webinars.

Canadianbfrb.org Another nonprofit organization. Look here for support groups across Canada and an online peer support system.

ChristinaPearson.com Christina offers courses in mindfulness-based stress reduction, specifically for BFRBs like skin picking.

Skinpickingsupport.com Angela Hartlin's website providing support and advocacy for those living with skin picking disorder.

Skinpick.com and **Stoppickingonme.com** These sites provide forums where you can interact with others.

Stoppicking.com - This is an interactive online program to help you make behavioral changes.

Secrets of Pulling and Picking - An app by Joan Kaylor. Available on iTunes and Android.

For EFT Tapping:

Emofree.com - Gary Craig's site with a free EFT tutorial.

Thetappingsolution.com - Nick and Jessica Ortner's popular site.

EFT Tapping for Dermatillomania video by Tammy Fletcher.

DrAmyMyers.com - A functional medicine M.D. who provides information on healing your gut, food sensitivities, and an excellent podcast.

DrMcCall.com - list of 75 health conditions benefited by yoga, including references to all the scientific studies

Helpful Books
Partly about skin picking:

Pearls: meditations on recovery from hair pulling and skin picking by Christina Sophia Pearson

The Habit Change Workbook: How to Break Bad Habits and Form Good Ones by James Claiborn, Ph.D., ABPP and Cherry Pedrick, R.N.

Skin Deep: A Mind/Body Program for Healthy Skin by Ted A Grossbart, Ph.D. And Carl Sherman, Ph.D.

A memoir about skin picking:

Forever Marked: A Dermatillomania Diary by Angela Hartlin

Other helpful books about topics in this book:

Overcoming Addictions by Deepak Chopra, M.D.

The Mood Cure and *The Diet Cure* by Julia Ross, M.A.

Change your Brain, Change your life by Daniel Amen, M.D.

Loving What Is by Byron Katie

Yoga as Medicine by Timothy McCall, M.D.

Ayurveda and the Mind by David Frawley, Ph.D.

Making the Brain/Body Connection by Sharon Promislow

The Promise of Energy Psychology by David Feinstein, Donna Eden and Gary Craig

Woman Heal Thyself by Jeanne Elizabeth Blum

Acknowledgments

I've been truly blessed with the opportunity to make my first unique book-length written contribution to the world. It is my sincere hope that this book will do much to heal and alleviate this particular brand of suffering.

Firstly, I want to give a big shout-out and thank you to my coaching clients, who allow me to witness the light of transformation again and again. You are all amazing people whom I am grateful to know.

I am indebted to Jennifer Raikes of the Trichotillomania Learning Center for her thorough critical reading of the manuscript. Jen's numerous suggestions made this a much better book than it would have been otherwise. Thanks also to Eric Yelsa and my dear friends Candace McClellan and Nat Damon, who all read an earlier version and provided helpful feedback and encouragement. Rose Scheltema helped with the EFT chapter and provided the picture of the tapping points. A lecture by Durga Leela informed and inspired the sense therapies chapter. Amy Friedman edited an earlier version of "the story of my skin picking" chapter while I worked on it in her memoir writing class.

Thank you to Tammy Fletcher for reading the book and contributing to the therapy chapter.

Juhi Kettry did better than read my mind when he designed the cover.

My heart is very grateful to Nicholas DeSomov for the love, partnership and unwavering support, plus help with the figures and final book cover edits.

I am grateful to all those who helped me get to the point of being able to write this book. The key ones I can think of: My therapy group leaders formerly at the OCD Center of LA: Maria Cervantes and Jon Hershfield. The founder of the Institute for Integrative Nutrition (IIN), Joshua Rosenthal, for the health coach training program without which I wouldn't have had a clue how to proceed. My teachers in the Sivananda Yoga organization, those I've learned from directly, but most especially to its founder, Swami Vishnudevananda, for bringing the teachings of yoga to the west, and to Swami Sivananda, who taught Swami Vishnu everything he (and we) need. Without the yogic practices to decrease my fear and increase my intuition, I know I wouldn't have made it to here. Thank you to my parents and grandparents and everyone else supporting me in this world or guiding me from beyond.

Notes

[1] Lissa Rankin, M.D. *Mind over medicine: scientific proof that you can heal yourself* (Carlsbad, CA: Hay House, Inc., 2013)

[2] Trichotillomania Learning Center (TLC) webinar on Mindfulness and BFRBs, 2014. Accessible to members of TLC.

[3] Monzani, B. et al. "Prevalence and heritability of skin picking in an adult community sample: a twin study" *Am J Med Genet B Neuropsychiatr Genet* 159B(5) 605-610 (2012)

[4] Grant, J.E. et al., "White matter abnormalities in skin picking disorder: a diffusor tensor imaging study," *Neuropsychopharmacology* 2013 Apr;38(5):763-9

[5] Schreiber, L., Odlaug, B.L., and Grant, J.E., "Impulse control disorders: updated review of clinical characteristics and pharmacological management," *Frontiers in Psychiatry*, 2 (2011) 1-11

[6] Keuthen, N. et al. "The prevalence of pathologic skin picking in US adults," *Compr. Psychiatry*, 51, 183-186

[7] Hayes, S.L., Storch, E.A. and Berlanga, L., "Skin picking behaviors: an examination of the prevalence and severity in a community sample." *J. Anxiety Disord.* 23, 314-319

[8] Odlaug, B.L. and Grant, J.E. (2012) Pathological skin picking. In *Trichotillomania, skin picking, & other body-focused repetitive behaviors* (pp. 21-41). Arlington, VA: American Psychiatric Publishing, Inc.

[9] Ibid.,34.

[10] Simeon, D. et al. "A double-blind trial of fluoxetine in pathologic skin picking," J. Clin. Psychiatry 58:341-347, 1997 and Bloch, M.R. et al.: "Fluoxetine in pathologic skin-picking: open-label and double-blind results," *Psychosomatics* 42: 314-319, (2001)

[11] Arbabi, M. et al. "Efficacy of citalopram in the treatment of pathological skin picking: a randomized double blind placebo controlled trial," *Acta Med Iran* 46: 367-372 (2008)

[12] Deckersbach, T. et al. "Cognitive-behavior therapy for self-injurious skin picking. A case series. *Behav modif.* 26(3): 361-377 (2002) and Teng, E.J., Woods, D.W., and Twohig, M.P. "Habit reversal as a treatment for chronic skin picking: a pilot investigation.

[13] Bloch, M.H. et al. "Systematic review: pharmacological and behavioral treatment for trichotillomania," *Biol Psychiatry* 62:839-846 (2007)

[14] Norman Doidge, M.D. *The brain that changes itself* (New York, NY: The Penguin Group, 2007)

[15] Wells, S. et al., "Evaluation of a meridian-based intervention, Emotional Freedom Techniques (EFT), for reducing specific phobias of small animals," *J Clin Psychol*, 59(9):943-966

[16] Church, D. et al, "Psychological trauma symptom improvement in veterans using emotional freedom techniques: a randomized controlled trial," *J Nerv Ment Dis* 201(2):153-160 (2013)

[17] Church, D., Yount, G. and Brooks, A.J., "The effect of emotional freedom techniques on stress biochemistry: a randomized controlled trial," *J Nerv Ment Dis*, 200(10):891-896 (2012)

[18] Basler, A.J., "Pilot study investigating the effects of Ayurvedic Abhyanga massage on subjective stress experience," *J Altern Complement Med* 17(5):435-440 (2011)

[19] Chevalier, G. et al. "Earthing: health implications of reconnecting the human body to the Earth's surface electrons," *J Environ Public Health* 291541 (2012)

[20] Clark, D.M., Salkovskis, P.M., Chalkley, A.J. "Respiratory control as a treatment for panic attacks," *J Behav There Exp Psychiatry* 16(1):23-30 (1985)

[21] Descilo, T. et al. "Effects of a yoga breath intervention alone and in combination with an exposure therapy for post-traumatic stress disorder and depression in survivors of the 2004 South-East Asia tsunami," *Acta Psychiatr Scand* 121(4):289-300 (2010)

[22] McCaul, K.D., Solomon, S., Holmes, D.S. "Effects of paced respiration and expectations on physiological and psychological responses to threat," *J Pers Soc Psychol* 37(4):564-571 (1979)

[23] Cappo, B.M. and Holmes, D.S. "The utility of prolonged respiratory exhalation for reducing physiological and psychological arousal in non-threatening and threatening situations," *J. Psychosomat. Res* 28:265-273 (1984)

[24] Kabat-Zinn, J. et al., "Effectiveness of a meditation-based stress reduction program in the treatment of anxiety disorders," *Am J Psychiatry* 149:936-943 (1992)

[25] Timothy McCall, M.D., *Yoga as Medicine* (New York, NY: Bantam Dell, 2007) and article with references on drmccall.com

[26] Deepak Chopra, M.D., *Overcoming Addictions: The Spiritual Solution* (New York, NY: Three Rivers Press, 1998)

[27] Woods, D.W. and Twohig, M.P., *Trichotillomania: An ACT-enhanced behavior therapy approach.* (New York, NY: Oxford University Press, 2008)

[28] Keuthen, N.J. et al, "Pilot trial of dialectical behavior therapy-enhanced habit reversal for trichotillomania," *Depress Anxiety* 27:953-959 (2010)

[29] Blumenthal, J.A. et al. "Effects of exercise training on older patients with major depression," *Arch Intern Med* 159(19):2349-2356 (1999)

[30] Penzel, F. *The hair pulling problem: a complete guide to trichotillomania* (New York, NY: Oxford University Press, 2003)

[31] Timothy McCall, M.D., *Yoga as Medicine* (New York, NY: Bantam Dell, 2007) and article with references on drmccall.com

[32] Robert H. Lustig, M.D. *Fat chance: beating the odds against sugar, processed food, obesity, and disease* (New York, NY: Hudson Street Press, 2012)

[33] Dufour, B.D. et al. "Nutritional up-regulation of serotonin paradoxically induces compulsive behavior," *Nutr Neurosci* 13(6) 256-264 (2010)

[34] Julia Ross, M.A., *The Diet Cure* (New York, NY: Penguin Group, 1999) p. 282 and references therein

[35] Julia Ross, M.A., *The Diet Cure* (New York, NY: Penguin Group, 1999)

[36] Spasov, A.A. et al, "Depression-like and anxiety-related behaviour of rats fed with magnesium-deficient diet," *Zh Vyss Nerv Deiat Im I P Pavlova* 58(4):476-485 (2008)

[37] Walton, R.G., Hudak, R., and Green-Waite, R.J., "Adverse reactions to aspartame: double-blind challenge in patients from a vulnerable population," *Biol Psychiatry* 34(1)13-17 (1993)

[38] A harrowing article on aspartame: http://www.huffingtonpost.com/robbie-gennet/donald-rumsfeld-and-the-s_b_805581.html

[39] Alvarez-Suarez, J.M., Giampieri, F. and Battino, M., "Honey as a source of dietary antioxidants: structures, bioavailability and evidence of protective effects against human chronic diseases," *Curr Med Chem*, 20(5):621-638 (2013) and Erejuwa, O.O., Sulaiman, S.A. and Wahab, M.S., "Honey - a novel antidiabetic agent," *Int J Biol Sci* 8(6):913-934 (2012)

[40] Fred Penzel, Ph.D., *The Hair-Pulling Problem* (New York, NY: Oxford University Press, 2003)

[41] Natasha Campbell-McBride, M.D., *Gut and Psychology Syndrome*, revised edition (Cambridge, UK: Medinform Publishing, 2010)

[42] http://www.mindbodygreen.com/0-7482/10-signs-youre-gluten-intolerant.html

[43] I think Amy Myers (dramymyers.com) is the best source of information online for this information.

[44] For lists of scientific studies of food additives on different conditions see www.feingold.org/research.php

[45] Study has not been published yet. It was presented at the 2013 American Diabetes Association meeting in Chicago.

[46] Blanchflower, D.G., Oswald, A.J. and Stewart-Brown, S., "Is psychological well-being linked to the consumption of fruit and vegetables?", *Soc Indic Res* 114:785-801 (2013)

[47] Peet, M. and Stokes, C., "Omega-3 fatty acids in the treatment of psychiatric disorders," *Drugs*, 65(8):1051-1059 (2005) and Ross, B.M., Seguin, J. and Sieswerda, L.E., "Omega-3 fatty acids as treatments for mental illness: which disorder and which fatty acid?" *Lipids Health Dis*, 6:21 (2007) and Cederholm, T. and Palmblad, J., "Are omega-3 fatty acids options for prevention and treatment of cognitive decline and dementia?" *Curr Opin Clin Nutr Metab Care*, 13(2):150-155 (2010)

[48] Pawlosky, R.J. et al., "Physiological compartmental analysis of alpha-linolenic acid metabolism in adult humans," *J Lipid Res*, 42(8):1257-65 (2001)

[49] http://www.mayoclinic.com/health/water/NU00283

[50] Kidd, P.M., "Omega-3 DHA and EPA for cognition, behavior, and mood: clinical findings and structural-functional synergies with cell membrane phospholipids," *Altern Med Rev* 12(3):207-227 (2007) and Schuchardt, J.P. et al., "Incorporation of EPA and DHA into plasma phospholipids in response to different omega-3 fatty acid formulations - a comparative bioavailability study of fish oil vs. krill oil," *Lipids Health Dis*, 10:145 (2011)

[51] Julia Ross, M.A., *The Mood Cure* (New York, NY: Penguin Group, 2002)

[52] Natasha Campbell-McBride, M.D., *Gut and Psychology Syndrome*, revised edition (Cambridge, UK: Medinform Publishing, 2010)

[53] Grant, J.E., Odlaug, B.L., Kim, S.W., "N-acetylcysteine, a glutamate modulator, in the treatment of trichotillomania: a double-blind, placebo-controlled study," *Arch Gen Psychiatry*, 66(7):756-763

[54] Fred Penzel, Ph.D. The hair-pulling problem: A complete guide to trichotillomania (New York, NY: Oxford University Press, 2003)

[55] Birdsall, T.C., "5-Hydroxytryptophan: a clinically effective serotonin precursor," *Altern Med Rev*, 3(4):271-280

[56] Weeks, B.S., "Formulations of dietary supplements and herbal extracts for relaxation and anxiolytic action: Relarian," *Med Sci Monit*, 15(11):RA256-262

[57] Steinberg, S., "A placebo-controlled study of the effects of L-tryptophan in patients with premenstrual dysphoria," *Adv Exp Med Biol*, 467:85-88 (1999)

[58] Fava, M. et al., "A double-blind, randomized trial of St. John's wort, fluoxetine, and placebo in major depressive disorder," *J Clin Psychopharmacol* 25(5):441-447

[59] Fish was found to have a protective effect against acne: Di Landro, A. et al. "Family history, body mass index, selected dietary factors, menstrual history, and risk of moderate to severe acne in adolescents and young adults," *J Am Acad Dermatol*, 67(6):1129-1135 (2012)

[60] Di Landro, A. et al. "Family history, body mass index, selected dietary factors, menstrual history, and risk of moderate to severe acne in adolescents and young adults," *J Am Acad Dermatol*, 67(6):1129-1135 (2012)

[61] Silverberg, N.B., "Whey protein precipitating moderate to severe acne flares in 5 teenaged athletes," *Cutis* 90(2):70-72 (2012)

[62] Melnik, B.C., "Diet in acne: further evidence for the role of nutrient signaling in acne pathogenesis," *Acta Derm Venereol* 92(3):228-231 (2012)

[63] Toyoda, M. and Morohashi, M., "New aspects in acne inflammation," *Dermatology* 206(1)17-23 (2003)

[64] Enshaieh, S. et al. "The efficacy of 5% topical tea tree oil gel in mild to moderate acne vulgaris: a randomized, double-blind placebo-controlled study," *Indian J Dermatol Venereol Leprol*, 73(1)22-25 (2007)

[65] Bassett, I.B., Pannowitz, D.L., Barnetson, R.S., "A comparative study of tea-tree oil versus benzoylperoxide in the treatment of acne," Med J Aust 153(8)455-458 (1990)

[66] Keuthen, N.J. et al. "The relationship of menstrual cycle and pregnancy to compulsive hairpulling," *Psychother Psychosom* 66(1):33-37 (1997)

[67] Jeanne Elizabeth Blum, M.T., O.M.T., *Woman heal thyself: An ancient healing system for contemporary women* (Boston, MA: Charles E Tuttle, Inc, 1995)

[68] Dr. Claudia Welch, MSOM, *Balance your hormones, balance your life: Achieving optimal health and wellness through Ayurveda, Chinese medicine and western science* (Cambridge, MA: De Capo Press, 2011)

24589994R00141

Made in the USA
San Bernardino, CA
29 September 2015